I0111023

The

Year

of the

Poet V

November 2018

The Poetry Posse

inner child press, ltd.

The Poetry Posse 2018

Gail Weston Shazor

Shareef Abdur Rasheed

Teresa E. Gallion

hülya n. yılmaz

Kimberly Burnham

Tzemin Ition Tsai

Elizabeth Esguerra Castillo

Jackie Davis Allen

Nizar Sartawi

Caroline 'Ceri' Nazareno

Ashok K. Bhargava

Alicja Maria Kuberska

Swapna Behera

William S. Peters, Sr.

General Information

The Year of the Poet V
November 2018 Edition
Series # 59

The Poetry Posse

1st Edition : 2018

Publisher Information
1st Edition : Inner Child Press
intouch@innerchildpress.com
www.innerchildpress.com

Copyright © 2018 : The Poetry Posse

ISBN-13 : 978-1-970020-65-6 (inner child press, ltd.)

$ 12.99

WHAT WOULD LIFE BE WITHOUT A LITTLE POETRY?

$\mathcal{D}$edication

This Book is dedicated to

Poetry . . .

The Poetry Posse

past, present & future

our Patrons and Readers

the Spirit of our Everlasting Muse

&

the Power of the Pen

to effectuate change!

In the darkness of my life
I heard the music
I danced. . .
and the Light appeared
and I dance

Janet P. Caldwell

Janet Perkins Caldwell

Rest In Peace

February 14, 1959 ~ September 20, 2016

Rest In Peace Dear Brother

Alan W. Jankowski

16 March 1961 ~ 10 March 2017

Poets . . .
sowing seeds in the
Conscious Garden of Life,
that those who have yet to come
may enjoy the Flowers.

Table of Contents

The Poetry Posse

Table of Contents . . . *continued*

November Featured Poets 99

Inner Child News 127

Other Anthological Works 145

foreword

Highland peaks

Since ancient times mountains have been arising human interest. Curiosity pushes daredevils to the tops covered with thick clouds. The enormity and majesty of the mighty rocky ridges intimidate and arouse fear but the harsh beauty of the mountain peaks acts like a magnet. Climbing up the summit and overcoming their own weaknesses have always led people to dangerous and steep mountain trails.

It is well known that the inspiration of poets originates from strong feelings and loveliness of nature. Mountains loom large in the cultural imagination. They exist in people's minds as much as they do on landscapes. The beauty and power of the mountains are described by words "to paint" landscapes. It happens that metaphors transfer their power and enormity to the other aspects of life.

There are many great verses dedicated to mountains. Their sublime majesty has inspired the best poets for ages . I will quote William Blake's dictum:

"Great things are done when men and mountains meet."

It is true. Readers can find a lot of beautiful poems about them. Let's read the poem written by Emily Dickinson.

"Ah, Teneriffe!"

Ah, Teneriffe!
Retreating Mountain!
Purples of Ages — pause for you —
Sunset — reviews her Sapphire Regiment —
Day — drops you her Red Adieu!

Still — Clad in your Mail of ices —
Thigh of Granite — and thew — of Steel —
Heedless — alike — of pomp — or parting

Ah, Teneriffe!
I'm kneeling — still —

"Ah Teneriffe", takes its inspiration from a mountain in the Canary Islands. In these poems, she is metaphorical mountaineer, grappling with the unimaginable power of mountains. Poetess attempts to achieve the summit of understanding. The mountain is transfigured into a fearsome warrior clad in icy armor to whom the royalty of this world — the "Purples of Ages" — defers. All she can do is bow in the mountain's presence and admire its beauty.

The nest poem is witten by by the Scottish poet William Renton. It appeared in his book of poetry

"Oils and Water Colours" and was published in 1893. He certainly paints a vivid picture in words of all the colours of a mountain twilight.

"Mountain Twilight"

The hills slipped over each on each
Till all their changing shadows died.
Now in the open skyward reach
The lights grow solemn side by side.
While of these hills the westermost
Rears high his majesty of coast
In shifting waste of dim-blue brine
And fading olive hyaline;
Till all the distance overflows,
The green in watchet and the blue
In purple. Now they fuse and close -
A darkling violet, fringed anew
With light that on the mountains soar,
A dusky flame on tranquil shores;
Kindling the summits as they grow
In audience to the skies that call,
Ineffable in rest and all
The pathos of the afterglow.

What about contemporary poetry? The answer you will find in this book...

Alicja Maria Kuberska

Poets, Writers . . . know that we are the enchanting magicians that nourishes the seeds of dreams and thoughts . . . it is our words that entice the hearts and minds of others to believe there is something grand about the possibilities that life has to offer and our words tease it forth into action . . . for you are the Poet, the Writer to whom the Gift of Words has been entrusted . . .

~ wsp

Preface

Dear Family and Friends,

Yes I am excited? Once again, this is an understatement! As we are hitting another milestone, the 11th month of our fifth year of publication . . . I am elated. Our initial vision was to just perform at this level for the year of 2014. Since that time we have had the blessed opportunity to include many other wonderful word artists and storytellers in the Poetry Posse from lands, cultures and persuasions all over the world. We have featured hundreds of additional poets, thereby introducing their poetic offerings to our vast global readership.

In keeping with our effort and vision to expand the awareness of poets from all walks by making this offerings accessible, we at Inner Child Press will continue to make every volume a FREE Download. The books are also available for purchase at the affordable cost of $7.00 per volume.

In the previous years, our monthly themes were Flowers, Birds, Gemstones and Trees. This year we have elected to take a different direction by theming our offerings after *Cultures* of past and present. In each month's volume you will have the opportunity to not only read at least one poem themed by our Poetry Posse members about such culture, but we have included a few words about the culture in our prologue. The reasoning behind this is that now our poetry has the opportunity to be educational for not only the reader, but we poets as well. We hope you find the poetic offerings insightful as we use our poetic form to relay to you what we too have learned through our research in making our offering available to you, our readership.

In closing, we would like to thank you for being an integral part of our amazing journey.

Enjoy our amazing featured poets . . . they are amazing!

Building Cultural Bridges of understanding . . .

Bless Up

From our house to yours

Bill
The Poetry Posse
Inner Child Press

PS

Do Not forget about the World Healing, World Peace Poetry effort.

Available here

www.worldhealingworldpeacepoetry.com

or

Janet . . . gone too soon.

http://www.innerchildpress.com/janet-p-caldwell.php

For Free Downloads of Previous Issues of The Year of the Poet

www.innerchildpress.com/the-year-of-the-poet

poetry is . . .

Highland Scotts

The **Highlands** (Scots: *the Hielands*; Scottish Gaelic: *A' Ghàidhealtachd* which translates to . . . "the place of the Gaels") is a historic region of Scotland. The area is very sparsely populated, with many mountain ranges dominating the region, and includes Ben Nevis, the highest mountain in the British Isles. Culturally, the Highlands and the Lowlands diverged from the later Middle Ages into the modern period, when Lowland Scots replaced Scottish Gaelic throughout most of the Lowlands.

The term "Highlands" is also used for the area north and west of the Highland Boundary Fault, although the exact boundaries are not clearly defined, particularly to the east.

For more information mgo to :
https://en.wikipedia.org/wiki/Scottish_Highlands

The
Year
of the
Poet V

November 2018

The Poetry Posse

inner child press, ltd.

Poetry succeeds where instruction fails.

~ wsp

Gail Weston Shazor

This is a creative promise ~ my pen will speak to and for the world. Enamored with letters and respectful of their power, I have been writing for most of my life. A mother, daughter, sister and grandmother I give what I have been given, greatfilledly.

Author of . . .

"An Overstanding of an Imperfect Love"
&
Notes from the Blue Roof

Lies My Grandfathers Told Me

available at Inner Child Press.

www.facebook.com/gailwestonshazor
www.innerchildpress.com/gail-weston-shazor
navypoet1@gmail.com

blessed rise

YWHW
i say YWHW from You
i breathe Your very name into my mouth
And the whisper covers the air i taste
You name yourself everlasting
Alpha and Omega
Am that you Am and
It is sufficient for my limitedness
And i breathe after You-Abah
In the midst of my day
In the middle of my life
i find that You are here
In the same place i find myself
It is not that You have ever left
i moved
And now that i have returned
i say yes
And draw close to You
For in this i am refined after my rescue
Storms rarely run in a straight line
And i have been buffeted around
And i have run headfirst into the wind
Even though You told me no
i could not hear for the listening
To my flesh senses
So my doxology has become this
i am greatfilled to the inked
And to the said
And to the whispered breath of You
i say yes to the wind across my face
The salty sea on my lips that flavors
My independence of dependence

For You are my choice
This one of abundant living in the midst
Of practicing to yield to You
i am your child of water
i am your adult of giving
i accept who You made me to be
So i live You in my waking
And in every love of my life
i expand, reach and fill much farther
Than i can ever hope to do alone
And though i am not perfect
You
Are

A Lovely City

At last in the lovely city
I remember nothing of rain
The sun never dims
Nor the moon rises
And it is always happy
At last in the lovely city
The bloom no longer surprises
For it is expected
To pull it's weight of hues
Without need of rosy glasses
At last in the lovely city
The wind is incapable of blowing
Up Marilyn's skirted whites
But only musters up
The unruffling light breezes
At last in the lovely city
My choices have been anticipated
And thinking is unnecessary
I only need to sit
In the gladness of metallicism
At last in this lovely city
Sometimes I become conscious
Of the scratching
At the base of my skull
And the rusting of truth
At last in this lovely city
There are no doors on rooms
And I have been told
That they are unnecessary
For there is no where left to go
(how much bleeding are we willing to do to maintain our
individuality)
The Rains

Will

There be
Children here
When the rains come
Back to the rice fields
And will they dance outside
Face toward the sumptuousness
That is always the beginning
That marks the season of hurricanes
Until too much rain chases us back inside

Alicja Maria Kuberska

.

Alicja Maria Kuberska – awarded Polish poetess, novelist, journalist, editor. She was born in 1960, in Świebodzin, Poland. She now lives in Inowrocław, Poland.
In 2011 she published her first volume of poems entitled: "The Glass Reality". Her second volume "Analysis of Feelings", was published in 2012. The third collection "Moments" was published in English in 2014, both in Poland and in the USA. In 2014, she also published the novel - "Virtual roses" and volume of poems "On the border of dream". Next year her volume entitled "Girl in the Mirror" was published in the UK and "Love me" , " (Not)my poem" in the USA. In 2015 she also edited anthology entitled "The Other Side of the Screen".

In 2016 she edited two volumes: "Taste of Love" (USA), "Thief of Dreams" (Poland) and international anthology entitled " Love is like Air" (USA). In 2017 she published volume entitled "View from the window" (Poland). She also edits series of anthologies entitled "Metaphor of Contemporary" (Poland)

Her poems have been published in numerous anthologies and magazines in Poland, the USA, the UK, Albania, Belgium, Chile, Spain, Israel, Canada, India, Italy, Uzbekistan, Czech Republic, South Korea and Australia. She was a featured poet of New Mirage Journal (USA) in the summer of 2011.

Alicja Kuberska is a member of the Polish Writers Associations in Warsaw, Poland and IWA Bogdani, Albania. She is also a member of directors' board of Soflay Literature Foundation.

Fall

I can see
people at the foot of the mountain
and those at its top
they have other desires and thoughts
a whole mountain
of incomprehension separates them

I notice
almost everyone wants to go higher
- over the borders of forest and fields
and climbs the rocks

and if it works
- lean the ladder against the clouds
lose sight of Earth
and be the only winner of this race

people forget that
falls from the summit
take place in loneliness
and are very painful

The Sun

When night ends, the show begins on the scene of sky.
The wind opens curtains made of clouds
- heavy and crimped like Baroque draperies.
 Birds begin to treble and proclaim the arrival of light.

Darkness disappears and night flies away on its black
wings.
The gray of morning slowly gains the pearly shades
and pink cloudlets lead the way on blue sky
for an oncoming solar chariot.

Digital Pharaoh
to the image of Mohamed Zakaria Soltan

Bits and bytes swirled, fuelled with colours,
and settled like droplets of rain on a piece of white paper.
Ancient gods of Egypt returned from the past.
The silhouettes of the powerful pharaohs emerged from the shadow
and the ancient world was born again of nothingness.

Anubis did not guard the fugitives from the Canyon Fields.
The beautiful Hathor showed them the way to the present day
and she opened the sealed gates of time.
The sons of Osiris came to Earth on Ra's papyrus boat.
Geb smiled happily at the sight of the reborn children.

Wise Thot, as always, helped humanity.
He collected moments lost in the desert sands
and he called vivid images from his memory
Faded colors became clear, blossoming brightly.
Expressive lines sketched the shapes of the former rulers.

Ascension of the blessed
to the image of Jerome Bosch

Man, leave everything
and go up towards the light.
Five stone circles separate you from the goal.
Here you can meet those who left earlier

Longing like a thin thread,
interwoven with memories,
connects this world and the time of the dead
They are waiting for you.

You have no meetings marked in your calendar
Important affairs scattered on the atoms
Take just a few steps and overcome the steep path
Eternity will open its gate for you

Alicja Maria Kuberska

Jackie

Davis

Allen

Jackie Davis Allen, otherwise known as Jacqueline D. Allen or Jackie Allen, grew up in the Cumberland Mountains of Appalachia. As the next eldest daughter of a coal miner father and a stay at home mother, she was the first in her family to attend and graduate from college. Her siblings, in their own right, are accomplished, though she is the only one, to date, that has discovered the gift of writing.

Graduating from Radford University, with a Bachelors of Science degree in Early Education, she taught in both public and private schools. For over a decade she taught private art classes to children both in her home and at a local Art and Framing Shop where she also sold her original soft sculptured Victorian dolls and original christening gowns.

She resides in northern Virginia with her husband, taking much needed get-aways to their mountain home near the Blue Ridge Mountains, a place that evokes memories of days spent growing up in the Appalachian Mountains.

A lover of hats, she has worn many. Following marriage to her college sweetheart, and as wife, mother, grandmother, teacher, tutor, artist, writer, poet and crafter, she is a lover of art and antiques, surrounding herself, always, with books, seeking to learn more.

In 2015 she authored *Looking for Rainbows, Poetry, Prose and Art*, and in 2017, *Dark Side of the Moon*. Both books of mostly narrative poetry were published by Inner Child Press and were edited by hulya n. yilmaz.

http://www.innerchildpress.com/jackie-davis-allen.php
jackiedavisallen.com

My Connection to the Highland Scots

The year that my ancestors came to North Carolina, USA,
is not yet known. But, I am a tartan leaf on two of the
Scottish ancestral trees: Campbell and Buchanan.

It is said that truth is stranger than fiction. In my case
it might be so, for had serendipity not played a part,
I'd not become who I am, nor penned this poem I've begun

My Campbell ancestor disappeared during the Civil War.
Thought to have been assassinated as a Confederate
sympathizer, along with others, he preparing to go north.

His widow Frye Campbell, left with a daughter, lonely,
sad, grieving, married a Davis widower. The widower's
younger brother had also died, serving in the Confederacy.

Paying his respects to his uncle, and his bride, I imagine,
he, the son of Davis' late brother, chanced upon the Frye
Campbell Davis' daughter. Uncle Davis' stepdaughter.

Nephew Davis and the daughter of the widow-bride Frye
Campbell Davis, had eleven children, one of whom was my
Davis grandfather. So, thank you, Highland Scots.

I haven't forgotten my Buchanan connection to the Scots.
My Davis grandfather married a Buchanan lass. He lived
to his mid 90s, and she, sadly, passed away in her mid 30s.

This poem did not start out nor end as I had supposed it
might have, but then, serendipity visits us in some of the
most interesting ways. Forgive me if I got a bit lost.

Crossing the River

Crossing the river
Towards a reawakening
The moon, in its fullness
Calls out to the stars
In their infancy

Beware of evil
Lurking in darkness
Hidden faces
In the shadows
They, the wicked

Sword of truth
Dwells within
Its path informs
Gift of love, of truth
Hint of peace

Why then
Do a people
Crossing over the river
Choose to hide
Civility, peace
From their faces

Defacement

Screams erupt
Like fire in eyes
Like pools
Of rubies crushed
Like voices mumbling
Hushed

Why is hate
So easily embraced
Come peace
Come with haste
Lest it be too late
To trust

Some old wounds
Reside visibly
Breaks my heart
Seeing innocent faces
Life too easily fading
Crushed

Tzemin Ition Tsai

Dr. Tzemin Ition Tsai (蔡澤民博士) was born in Tzemin Ition Tsai Taiwan, Republic of China, in 1957. He holds a Ph.D. in Chemical Engineering and two Masters of Science in Applied Mathematics and Chemical Engineering. He is an associate professor at the Asia University (Taiwan), editor of "Reading, Writing and Teaching" academic text. He also writes the long-term columns for Chinese Language Monthly in Taiwan.

He is a scholar with a wide range of expertise, while maintaining a common and positive interest in science, engineering and literature member.

He has won many national literary awards. His literary works have been anthologized and published in books, journals, and newspapers in more than 40 countries and have been translated into more than a dozen languages.

The Song Always Weeping as The Sun Is Going Down

Time always seems rushed and precise.
I couldn't help but watch the sun go down the mountain.
Like this highland,
Towering into the sky along the edge of the sea.
What kind of sound of nature will forget the warning.
Mother was gradually drifting away
Yes, she will does eventually leave.
The song that should sound when the sun sets.
Keep silent.

Wind blowing over the farm.
Did not stop playing.
Why did I only hear the sound of the treetops?
Scratching my heart
Scratching my innermost being
Never asked me about the scars left behind
When to fix?
Naturally, you won't ask.
Facing a delicate and frail girl like me.

A loving marriage,
Why was it so unbearable and fragile?
Tribulation of war, lingering shadow of death,
Forced to take everything away.
Why was everything so pale in my dreams?
But everything in everything,
the very thought of
That kiss has never been realized.
Until the last time we met.

The Napping Old Cat

That old lane after a long time for renovation
A stunning new look appears
One million years of indifference
Those cracked floor tiles in yellowed clothes
The moss trying to climb up the wall
All were eradicated
Obviously
Got a fair compromise with time
After wearing new color coats
Finally, it could radiantly talk with the walls on both sides
Only that old cat squatting on the wall under the afternoon
sun
Continued to nap
That kind of silent look
Just waiting
To see
How long can you stay bright?

I'm The Peacock King

The sky
Misty black
Soul buried deep in the forest trying to find a way out
Half Flapping and half climbing
To reach the top of my wooden house
Sound attacking on the top of the hill
Standing alone with one foot Just like a proud peacock
should do
This seat
No man alive can take away
Hel! Hel! Hel!

Choose an angle as a feudal lord
Let
The first dawn
Shoot at my crown
Until my crown red through and through
My wings that have fully opened now
I looked at that group of mortals under my feet with
contempt
Swallowing a full mouth of worshipped wine
My head lifts up until it's too high
Hel! Hel! Hel!

Why you all stare at me in this way
Do I
need to be just like you
To pick up
That few rice left in the grain tank
Pooh
Do not pretend that you can't hear anything
My cry forever and always
loud
Hel! Hel! Hel!

Shareef
Abdur
Rasheed

Shareef Abdur-Rasheed, AKA Zakir Flo was born and raised in Brooklyn, New York. His education includes Brooklyn College, Suffolk County Community College and Makkah, Saudi Arabia. He is a Veteran of the Viet Nam era, where in 1969 he reverted to his now reverently embraced Islamic Faith. He is very active in the Islamic community and beyond with his teachings, activism and his humanity.

Shareef's spiritual expression comes through the persona of "Zakir Flo" . Zakir is Arabic for "To remind". Never silent, Shareef Abdur-Rasheed is always dropping science, love, consciousness and signs of the time in rhyme.

Shareef is the Patriarch of the Abdur-Rasheed Family with 9 Children (6 Sons and 3 Daughters) and 41 Grandchildren (24 Boys and 17 Girls).

For more information about Shareef, visit his personal FaceBook Page at :

https://www.facebook.com/shareef.abdurrasheed1
https://zakirflo.wordpress.com

Up in NorthWest..,

Scotland called Highlands
roamed the clans whose home
was in those vast, isolated,
sparsely populated
highlands
salt of earth, poor struggle
from birth to return into
dirt
remained the crofters
farming patches of land
in vast
Scottish northwest
highlands
struggle in name of survival
these Scottish Gaelic speaking
clans cut from the often unforgiven
land
so, they did what they can in their
nation
though many choose migration
to places far away
in name of survival
lives sought revival, cross seas
in places like British and American
cities
or joined British armies
in name of survival
for them often life in the Highlands
was not kind
though they tried, endured remain
through the pain
maintain the ways they knew

stay strong, true
yes, nothing new
peoples of earth do
what they must do
in name of survival

food4thought = education

Reflecting..,

on dem who reflect
bigups, respect
word sculptors
creative souls cut from
carefully woven rolls,
of fabric rare
manifested in sublime
rhyme, rhythm, prose
like Rakim i say
"let the rhythm hit em"
profound skill dem who
paint with words at will
who has profound
love beyond the pale
outside the box
what resides inside prevails
dem special folk provoke
introspective jubilees
such is the souls that delve
far below where others dare
not go
in places deep seeded
concepts grow out of
questions
demand answers
to mysteries that life holds
poets possess demanding souls
thirst and hunger to know

(Just Bill on my mind)
Dedicated: William S. Peters Sr.

food4thought = education

night's darkness..,

descended
they thought it was light
thinking wrong is right
day is night
darkness descends upon us
like a plague
turning from enlightenment
to ignorance instead
where daylight enhances life
nights darkness invites death
in the form of.,
blind, dumb, deaf
is all the rage for now
until the day it erupts in flames
and goes away somehow
as the light of truth takes
the stage and bows
as mother earth screams more
and light of truth takes
encore after encore
but for today we defer
to the master playwright
and you know only he knows
how to write the play right
the creator, life's originator
knows what we know not
until then this is how it flows
my friend as the devil stirs
the pot
folk who think they know
say what it is and it's not
leaving truth behind

because without guidance
divine
lose their dam mind
dem think ignorance is bliss
perception distorted
what's this..,
knowledge, wisdom aborted?
prophecy fulfilled as originally
reported
ignorance will be flaunted
while knowledge and wisdom
disappear without a trace
ignorance walks in and takes
its place
then honor replaced with disgrace
now is that time, here is that place

food4thought = education

Kimberly Burnham

See yourself in the pattern. As a 28-year-old photographer, Kimberly Burnham appreciated beauty. Then an ophthalmologist diagnosed her with a genetic eye condition saying, "Consider life, if you become blind." She discovered a healing path with insight, magnificence, and vision. Today, a poet and neurosciences expert with a PhD in Integrative Medicine, Kimberly's life mission is to change the global face of brain health. Using health coaching, Reiki, Matrix Energetics, craniosacral therapy, acupressure, and energy medicine, she supports people in their healing from nervous system and chronic pain issues. A current project is taking pages from medical literature and turning them into visual poetry by circling the words of the poem and coloring in the rest—recycling words into color and drawing out the poem.

http://www.NerveWhisperer.Solutions
https://www.linkedin.com/in/kimberlyburnham

Scottish Men of Peace

The fairies of the Scottish Highlands
politely spoken of as the "Daoine Síth"
"Men of Peace"
wander through mythology
healing the world with magic

The "aos sí" or the older form "aes sídhe"
Irish for a supernatural race
fairies and elves
weave our way into Scottish mythology
spelled "sìth" wishing peace for mankind

W. B. Yeats refers to "aos sí"
simply as "the sídhe"
we live underground in fairy mounds
across the western sea
an invisible world
coexists with the world of humans

This world described
in the Lebor Gabála Érenn
a parallel universe finds the "aos sí" walking
among the living
the ancestors
the spirits of nature
of goddesses and gods

Always in peace "sìth" in Scottish Gaelic
"sìoth" in the dialect of Ulster and Northern Ireland
where people and fairies alike wish
for "sìoth on irth"

Peace in Seven Celtic Nations

In the Ancient Celtic of Cornwall
"hedh" is peace and tranquility
feasible easy and free from difficulty
as if in Kernow spoken in Cornwall
life is doable only if there is peace
said also "cres" or "kres"
"yn clôr" or "yn cosel" or "drê gosoleth"
peaceably in this descendant
of an Ancient British language
before English came to dominate

"Síth" or "síthe" or "sod" peace
"síocháin" the way of peace
in Gaeilge or Irish Gaelic
words in Ireland or Eire
"sítheach" peaceful and harmonious
"sítheach sóch" peaceful and comfortable
while "go sítheach grách" is harmony and love
peace begetting harmony comfort and ultimately love

"Sìth" peace in Scottish Gaelic
also called Alba the dialect of Scotland
"peace" in English
and "fois" means relaxation tranquility
ease repose respite
a loan word from Scottish
in Nova Scotia
Canada's New Scotland
where this smallest of provinces
includes Cape Breton and 3,800 coastal islands

Far across the sea on the Isle of Mann
"shee" is the way peace said

in Gaelg or Manx Gaelic
the native language of this island
called Ellan Vannin in the Irish Sea
between Britain and Ireland
where we speak a Gaelic language
related to Irish or Gaeilge
and Scots Gaelic or Gàidhlig
spelled closer to English style

"Eaz" or "aez" is feasible
easy and free from difficulty in Amoric
or the Breton of French Brittany
where we spell peace many ways
"peoc'h" "pèc'h" "peoh" "peuc'h"
or "diskuizh" in France's northwestern most region
where the pink granite coast is famed
for unusual blush-hued sand and rocks
known for an abundance of prehistoric "menhirs"

Harkening back to the Ancient Celtic of Cornwall
peace in this land is said "heddwch" or "hawdh" or "hedh"
in Welsh "héz" means that which glides onward
peace calm tranquility
as if peace is a lubricant that makes people move
towards each other and closer to "thawelwch"
another way of peace and quiet
in this language called Cymraeg
spoken in Wales or Cymru

"Koňiben" is a Traveler's word for peace and quiet
in Welsh Romani also called Kååle
influenced by languages far flung
as Hindustani and the Celtic Welsh
a language of the Traveler people in Wales
"dootchiparen" is peace or "piratchi"

in Angloromani or British Isles Romani
as words of peace caravan across the lands and seas

Long ago to Galicia in northwest Spain
today considered the seventh of the original Celtic Nations
influenced by Spanish and Portuguese
in Galician we say "paz"
wishing for peace in the Celtic world and beyond

Brio Celtic Power

"Brio" a word in Galician
means might or power
showing Latin and Celtic influences in Spain

"Brio" power and might in Italian
comes from the Catalan or Old Occitan "briu" wild
from Celtic "brigos"
a cognate of Occitan "briu"

Old French "brif" means finesse or style
akin to Old Irish "bríg" or power
and the Welsh "bri" prestige and authority
or the Breton "bri" respect

So it seems power and respect
go together with a wild style
unique and prestigious
yet rooted in history and forward looking

To what this Galician community
we build with our power and might
the kind of peace or "paz"
we support

Can we write in Celtic stone "kalyāwo"
and move "callao" Galician boulders or pebbles
are there obstacles to peace
written in "kalyāwo"
are they as big as a boulder
is it just perspective
they are small like a pebble
descended from stones
and strength

Where will we find the path to "paz"
the Galician "camiño"
the way or path from Vulgar Latin "cammīnus"
and Proto-Celtic "kanxsman"
same as or a cognate of Italian "cammino"
French "chemin"
Spanish "camino"
Catalan "camí"
Occitan "camin"
akin to the Old Irish "céimm"
Cornish and Breton "kamm" or step

We look for peace
helping neighbors along the way
no matter what we say
the words we use just remnants
of the history we share
the power of a helping hand
needs no translation

Elizabeth E. Castillo

Elizabeth Esguerra Castillo is a multi-awarded and an Internationally-Published Contemporary Author/Poet and a Professional Writer / Creative Writer / Feature Writer / Journalist / Travel Writer from the Philippines. She has 2 published books, "Seasons of Emotions" (UK) and "Inner Reflections of the Muse", (USA). Elizabeth is also a co-author to more than 60 international anthologies in the USA, Canada, UK, Romania, India. She is a Contributing Editor of Inner Child Magazine, USA and an Advisory Board Member of Reflection Magazine, an international literary magazine. She is a member of the American Authors Association (AAA) and PEN International.

Web links:

Facebook Fan Page

https://free.facebook.com/ElizabethEsguerraCastillo

Google Plus

https://plus.google.com/u/0/+ElizabethCastillo

Travel to Highland Scots

A young Scots lass is out to find a beloved who will
    embrace her
One fine day, The Knights Templar escaped to Scotland,
She met the young man from the ward of the Master of the
Temple The men brought with them some treasure,
And in exchange may marry women from the clans.

I'd like to wander around the castle,
Of the Dowager Countess in the highlands
Built in the 14th century by William, 3rd Thane of Cawdor,
Immerse myself with its antiquity and mysterious history
A melting pot of excellent aesthetic for contemporary art.

To be in a different fortress, the Dunnottar Castle,
Or perhaps tour the Carbisdale Castle, "the castle of spite"
Within these highlands, history and grandeur alight,
The epics: Outlander, James Bond, and Highlander
Were all filmed in this land where earth and sky meet.

Bridge

Crossing to the other side
Would thy soul ease its thirst?
As the moon wax and wanes
Would I enter a threshold
Of utter peace and no ounce of pain?
A voice whispered to me,
Go on and walk over, follow the shadow
You'd then discover the beauty of yonder
The magical bridge, gateway to a new world,
Where your spirit can roam free.

She entered another dimension,
Angelic symphony, soft, velvet and liquid gold
Her departed ones came into vision
As the voice prompted her to let go,
 Experience love like never before.

The nectar that feeds one's soul,
With the infinite wisdom of the Great Spirit Led her to a
special bridge,
That moment changed her life around
Let Divine Energy within her flow.

Sunset

The dreamy sunset at the distant horizon
When dusk settles as the sun bids adieu,
Extinguishing the light to make way
For the darkness and let the moon reign- Casting shadows
of red and orange hues.

The blazing heat which once was burning,
Turned into pale madness when cold breeze sets in
A life-size canvass above can be seen,
Lovers sitting by the shoreline Witnessing the grandeur of a
Divine Masterpiece.

Deafening silence- Beating hearts can only be heard
Seagulls flying- Stories foretold of a thousand years of
waiting
Souls keep meeting beyond time and space.

 You and I- Thy names shall be called eternally,
And in every sunset, I'll wait by the sea Even in secrecy-
For each day starts and ends with a love,
That's only meant for you.

Nizar Sartawi

Nizar Sartawi is a poet, translator, essayist, and columnist. He was born in Sarta, Palestine, in 1951. He is a member of literary and cultural organizations, including the Jordanian Writers Association (Jordan), General Union of Arab Writers (Cairo), Poetry Posse (U.S.), Inner Child Press International (U.S.), Bodgani (Belgium), and Axlepin Publishing (the Philippines). He has participated in poetry readings and international forums and festivals in numerous countries, including Jordan, Lebanon, Kosovo, Palestine, Morocco, Egypt, and India. Sartawi's poems have been translated into several languages. His poetry has been anthologized and published in many anthologies, journals, and newspapers in Arab countries, the U.S., Australia, Indonesia, Bosnia, Italy, India, the Philippines, and Taiwan.

Sartawi has published more than 20 books of poetry and poetry translation. His last poetry collection, *My Shadow,* was published in June, 2017 by Inner Child Press in the U.S.

For the last seven years, Sartawi has been working on poetry translation from English to Arabic and Arabic to English. This includes his Arabic poetry translation project, "Arab Contemporary Poets Series" in which 13 bilingual books have been published so far. He also has translated poems for a number of contemporary international poets such as, Veronica Golos, Elaine Equi; William S. Peters; Kalpna Singh-Chitnis; Nathalie Handal, Naomi Shihab Nye; Candice James; Ashok Bhargava; Santiago Villafania, Virginia Jasmin Pasalo; Rosa Jamali; Taro Aizu; Fahredin Shehu, and many others.

Highland Clearances

Wave after wave
they were expelled
by their own chiefs

out of the small dry-stone
blackhouses
that sheltered them in the rough terrains
of Scottish Highlands

out of the farmlands
that they tilled
with their own tough
cracked hands

out of the steep hills
that they shared with fellow crofters
as grazing lands.

Oh how their forlorn faces
dissolved
among the masses
in the brave
new world
leaving behind
the resonances of their lore –
the Gaelic songs and tunes
the beats of their tenor drums
the shrill sounds of their Great bagpipes
the rustling of their kilts and tartans
as they danced their proud
sword dances –
reverberating amidst the straths and glens
that witnessed their highland feasts
and loud revelries!

A Perpetual Nightmare

She woke up in the middle
of again the same nightmare
a long queue
of disfigured ghosts
the children men and women
of her city – Gaza –
moving sluggishly
before her eyes
and turning into
purplish ash…

Her wrinkled face
sweating
she sinks
beneath the quilt
and like a brittle jar
she breaks
into tears…

Diabolic Truce

This time
the Synagogue and the Mosque
were resolutely reconciled:

They both agreed…
YES *They Agreed*
it was a great offense
for this young Jewess
to be in love
with that young Arab from Palestine
or that same Arab
to be in love
with this same Jewess.

Mosque and Synagogue
concurred without hesitancy
that
it was a deadly sin…
A Deadly Sin
for this Arab
and that Jewess
to be wedded,
a deadly sin for them
to live under a single roof,
a deadly sin
to share one bed,
a deadly sin to kiss
to touch
to talk
or even wave,

that at all costs
this
Will Not BE…

Self-willed,
the young couple eloped
to seek asylum
in the Church
they knocked and knocked
on the locked church gate
One click…
and the gate was now securely
double-locked.

The Denouement:
Two corpses lying on the ground
facing the open space
trying to make
some sense
out of a senseless world!

to be continued… in the afterworld.

hülya

n.

yılmaz

Born in Turkey, hülya n. yılmaz presently serves as full-time faculty at Penn State and as the Director of Editing Services at Inner Child Press. Her academic publications dwell on literary relations between the West and the Islamic East and on gender conceptualizations within the context of Islam. Dr. yılmaz had her formal initiation as a creative writer in the U.S. Her published works include *Trance* –a tri-lingual book of poetry, *Aflame* –memoirs in verse and *An Aegean Breeze of Peace* –a poem collection she has co-authored with Demetrius Trifiatis. Poetry by hülya appeared in excess of fifty international anthologies.

hülya n. yılmaz, Ph.D.

Links

Personal Web Site
https://hulyasfreelancing.com

Personal Blog Site
https://dolunaylaben.wordpress.com/

The Highland Fling

i feel like dancing again
as i often do
for this one however
i must have you

i do not play the accordion
would you mind us switching the roles
i will go ahead and do The Highland Fling
this way we'll still fill the gender holes

i confess in broad daylight yes i openly do
this mountainous rocky terrain and harsh winters
make me wince for a lifetime even two
the makeshift floor gives me too many splinters

let's forget our Campbells, McNeills and Stewarts
our world-famous Presbyterian churches too
we'd be better off in a North Carolina colony
this Highland Fling gets to be too much of an ado

Gaelic

we all moved to the Cape Fear River today
our largest settlement in North America
along with us came our native tongue
its mark is left in many churches they say
but most of all in Hoke County
"Dundarrach" – "hill of the oak tree"
remained in the new language as the same
North Carolina's Provincial Congress
had even made a noteworthy address
to accurately and justifiably stress
the due distinction importance and the extent
to which Gaelic resisted to have a premature end
the year was 1776 you see
what a time it was for a High Scotlander to be!

The "Kintail bard"

i already said i wanted to dance today
my desire was met by the dear John MacRae
in case you want to know about him a bit
he was in North Carolina before the war fires were lit
the Revolutionary War that is
he was known as a true Loyalist
though his fate is still a mystery
several of his songs made history
his "Dean Cadalan Samhach" was a true hit
"Sleep Softly, My Darling Beloved"
is said to have become its adopted name
the myth is that he owes his persistent fame
to Highland Scots' culture's oral tradition frame

Teresa E. Gallion

Teresa E. Gallion was born in Shreveport, Louisiana and moved to Illinois at the age of 15. She completed her undergraduate training at the University of Illinois Chicago and received her master's degree in Psychology from Bowling Green State University in Ohio. She retired from New Mexico state government in 2012.

She moved to New Mexico in 1987. While writing sporadically for many years, in 1998 she started reading her work in the local Albuquerque poetry community. She has been a featured reader at local coffee houses, bookstores, art galleries, museums, libraries, Outpost Performance Space, the Route 66 Festival in 2001 and the State of Oklahoma's Poetry Festival in Cheyenne, Oklahoma in 2004. She occasionally hosts an open mic.

Teresa's work is published in numerous Journals and anthologies. She has two CDs: *On the Wings of the Wind* and *Poems from Chasing Light*. She has published three books: *Walking Sacred Ground, Contemplation in the High Desert* and *Chasing Light.*

Chasing Light was a finalist in the 2013 New Mexico/Arizona Book Awards.

The surreal high desert landscape and her personal spiritual journey influence the writing of this Albuquerque poet. When she is not writing, she is committed to hiking the enchanted landscapes of New Mexico. You may preview her work at

http://bit.ly/1aIVPNq or http://bit.ly/13IMLGh

Modern Highlands

The Highland Scots make claims
to the impressive Scottish landscape.
Ben Nevis peak sits high in the sky
offering a grand view of the land.

You boast unspoiled rugged mountains,
deep blue lakes and glens
where majestic Eagles rule the skies
and red deer roam the valley.

Legends of a Loch Ness monster
that lives in the deep waters
of the Loch Ness lake are told
over Scotch whiskey in the pubs.

Travelers come to experience
Gaelic culture, drink your famous
whiskey, drive your scenic byways,
boat on your waters and hike your trails.

Swiss Girls

The hills are alive with bells
and sexy girls with flirtatious walks
doing a fashion run on the mountainside.

Milk chocolate, blackberry and
vanilla/chocolate mixes eat
with focus and intent while the bells

play love songs to happy healthy cows.
The sweet Alp grass nourishes bellies.
A gift of milk comes from nipple massages.

The life of a swiss cow is charmed.
Some of the girls chill out re-chewing food
in the luxury of Swiss mountain majesty.

Swiss Alps

Words elude me as my eyes feast
on the grandeur of these mountains.
Did I die and go to heaven?

My soul aches with joy
with each step I take.
Ecstatic bliss makes me tremble
as my boots engage the trail.

My legs freeze as I look out
on the Master's priceless canvas.
Nothing and no one may come close
to the splendor caressing my eyes.

I just want to drop to my knees,
say thank you for the experience
stroking my heartstrings.

Ashok K. Bhargava

Ashok Bhargava is a poet, writer, community activist, public speaker, management consultant and a keen photographer. Based in Vancouver, he has published several collections of his poems: Riding the Tide, Mirror of Dreams, A Kernel of Truth, Skipping Stones, Half Open Door and Lost in the Morning Calm. His poetry has been published in various literary magazines and anthologies.

Ashok is a Poet Laureate and poet ambassador to Japan, Korea and India. He is founder of WIN: Writers International Network Canada. Its main objective is to inspire, encourage, promote and recognize writers of diverse genres, artists and community leaders. He has received many accolades including Nehru Humanitarian Award for his leadership of Writers International Network Canada, Poets without Borders Peace Award for his journeys across the globe to celebrate peace and to create alliances with poets, and Kalidasa Award for creative writings.

The Wall

the sky's uniform
less than cosmic
with the confusion of morning mist
over new willow catkins

drink some more wine
other side of Hadrian wall
you may not know anyone
in the land of Gaels

above the Highlands
a blooming midnight moon
brushes a glowing
across the rivers and valleys

Romans built the wall
to keep invading Scots
the barbarians from migrating
smuggling or stealing sheep

but they loved highland maidens
red lips
accented tongues
blushing cheeks

they gave them wine
in golden goblets
to drink all they wanted
behind the wall in dark

with no way to articulate
their bones felt good
after making love
and not being loved

Invisible Hope

My prayers are folded hands
holding silence.
In the darkness of night
I search for the spirit of invocations.

It sparks deep desire in me
to oscillate from eternity to infinity.

Light shines on silently
bringing peace to distressed heart.

My body is fragile glass
shatters easily.
My resolve is stronger than steel
unbreakable.

Without waiting for an avatar -
I sow a seed of hope
when it sprouts
blossoms would be me.

Soft Touch

If you wish to love me
then accept me as I am
and nothing else.

If you like to trust me
then believe in me
for no reason at all.

If you want to caress me
then touch me with your eyes
without asking why.

Because one day
my love will spring
my passion will emerge
my heart will blossom and
my zeal will grow
for you.

But if you cannot wait for me
then without any hesitation
leave me and go away.

Because I can create you
when I am ready.

Caroline
'Ceri Naz'
Nazareno

Caroline Nazareno-Gabis a.k.a. Ceri Naz, born in Anda, Pangasinan known as a 'poet of peace and friendship', is a multi-awarded poet, journalist, editor, publicist, linguist, educator, and women's advocate.

Graduated cum laude with the degree of Bachelor of Elementary Education, specialized in General Science at Pangasinan State University. Ceri have been a voracious researcher in various arts, science and literature. She volunteered in Richmond Multicultural Concerns Society, TELUS World Science, Vancouver Art Gallery, and Vancouver Aquarium.

She was privileged to be chosen as one of the Directors of Writers Capital International Foundation (WCIF), Member of the Poetry Posse, one of the Board of Directors of Galaktika ATUNIS Magazine based in Albania; the World Poetry Canada and International Director to Philippines; Global Citizen's Initiatives Member, Association for Women's rights in Development (AWID) and Anacbanua. She has been a 4th Placer in World Union of Poets Poetry Prize 2016, Writers International Network-Canada ''Amazing Poet 2015'', The Frang Bardhi Literary Prize 2014 (Albania), the sair-gazeteci or Poet-Journalist Award 2014 (Tuzla, Istanbul, Turkey) and World Poetry Empowered Poet 2013 (Vancouver, Canada).

Caledonia

Scottish Love, that must be the song
While the curtain laces afterimages
Bathing the tongues, diffusions of change
Writing in braille from innermost quench
Yet, it has to see you withstand
Eavesdropping crossroads
Filling in the whys
of timeless ballads
Will meet in the homecoming
at Glasgow's winding mountain thymes,
The Rhymes of inamorata.

Aberdeen and Promises

Crystal clear that was
While bathing on the
Sunset's kisses
Where ponds, rivers
And lakes of love
Took away the flaws,
Your heart is the sunshine
To eternity's quest;
That single day
Was a world
Of ours, my love, forever.

Scottish Wine

Be mine tonight.
In my vineyard
Of flowers, berries and leaves,
Sweet and bittersweet spells
From your lips,
As we burn the night
And free the moonlit concoction
Together we'll drink
Over the cobblestone table
Enjoying the bizarre taste
While it last, 'til the picturesque battle.

Swapna Behera

Swapna Behera is a bilingual contemporary poet, author, translator and editor from Odisha, India.She was a teacher from 1984 to 2015 . Her stories, poems and articles are widely published in National and International journals, and ezines, and are translated into different national and International languages. She has penned four books. She was conferred upon the Prestigious International Poesis Award of Honor at the 2nd Bharat Award for Literature as Jury in 2015, The Enchanting Muse Award in India World Poetree Festival 2017, World Icon of Peace Award in 2017, and the Pentasi B World Fellow Poet in 2017.. She is the recipient of Gold Cross Of Wisdom Award ,the medal for The Best Teachers of the World from World Union of Poets in 2018, and The LIfe time Achievement Award ,The Best Planner Award and The Sahitya Shiromani Award from the Literati Cosmos Society 2018 .She is the Ambassador of Humanity by Hafrikan Prince Art World,Africa 2018 and an official member of World Nation's Writers Union ,Kazakhstan2018. At present she is the manager at Large, Planner and Columnist of The Literati and the administrator of several poetic groups

In Search Of The Best God.....

Someone whispers
May be asking water to drink
Air to breathe
Sky to see the stars
A roof on the head
Or little soil to keep his feet

Someone whispers
Who is the best God?
Listening to tears
Sweeping all fears
Someone somewhere
Sings lullaby for a baby

Perhaps the best God is awake
 Dreams light for all
Breaks the shackle
Fixes the fractured democracy
Opens all doors
Weaves life
Descends down to the hearts
Holding the gift of a Sun
For you and for me

Yes the best God is screaming
For He wishes
In condensed intensity
 to be a human- being
And my search is over !!!!

Epilogue Of A Bagpiper

Give me a heart
I will sing
Give me a boat
I will sail across the placid lakes
Echoes the Urlar
In the distant island of
Scottish high land
The haggis is ready for the
Grand festival of Hogmanay
the smokes raising high up
the Unicorn grazing
in the   valley
 No more old trees
but the gregarious roots
still holding underneath
the radiant history
The cascade
Still crazy with ardent rhymes
  I am ready with my unfurled tunes
Give me a heart to blow.....
All fragrances ......

Shadow In The Vortex

The vivisection started
May be the interactive Viva-voce
The shadow was jumping
Playing merry-go-round
Smiling and shaking hands
Everything was normal

The shadow with its length and breadth
Searching for the volume
Where is it ?
Beneath the slumbering eyelid ?
Or browsing in the cosmos to get a dialect
A music to overcome the labyrinth

My shadow ! Alas, my dear shadow
Caged in my bones
And the body jumping
from the time table to anatomy table
Ready for dissection!!!

William S.
Peters Sr.

Bill's writing career spans a period of over 50 years. Being first Published in 1972, Bill has since went on to Author in excess of 40 additional Volumes of Poetry, Short Stories, etc., expressing his thoughts on matters of the Heart, Spirit, Consciousness and Humanity. His primary focus is that of Love, Peace and Understanding!

Bill says . . .

I have always likened Life to that of a Garden. So, for me, Life is simply about the Seeds we Sow and Nourish. All things we "Think and Do", will "Be" Cause and eventually manifest itself to being an "Effect" within our own personal "Existences" and "Experiences" . . . whether it be Fruit, Flowers, Weeds or Barren Landscapes! Bill highly regards the Fruits of his Labor and wishes that everyone would thus go on to plant "Lovely" Seeds on "Good Ground" in their own Gardens of Life!

to connect with Bill, he is all things Inner Child

www.iaminnerchild.com

Personal Web Site

www.iamjustbill.com

Breathe

These hills are mine and thine
My laddy

Our fathers,
And our father before them
Have nurtured these lands
With their Blood
Sweat
And tears

There are more years to come
Than what we have spent
Hold to the promise

We have tilled this land
With purpose,
With a certain freedom
Throughout
Many a season,
Many a year . . .
Raised our stock,
Our children,
And our families . . .
This is your inheritance

Can not you hear the music
Of our forefathers
Dancing,
Playing in between
The whispers
Of the winds

O laddy
Just close thine eyes
And open thy heart
To the way of the Scotts
And feel your Gay-like
Bonny
Bright
Gaelic
Blood coursing
As one
With we the people
Of these highlands

Breathe

Muse

She seemingly surreptitiously slithered
Silently into my solace soaked
Consciousness
Tickling, stimulating
My wonder and curiosity

She wanted to play
And I wanted to sleep
But that would not be,
For she had a poem
She wanted to give to me . . .

I am waiting

Observing

It was a time
That was not quite
Understood

There were psychic
Movings
Dancing in my thoughts
Prodding my spirit
To awaken . . . keenly

Was I contemplating
Without subject? . . .
What was my objective ?

I sat, I listened,
I reached
For that elusive
Glistening epiphany

The realm of
Circumspection,
Introspection,
Reflection,
Gave unto no
Detection
In this state
Of abyss
Where naught but void
Exists

Was I seeking . . .
Bliss
Of peace

Just observing

November

2018

Features

~ * ~

Michelle Joan Barulich

Monsif Beroual

Krystyna Konecka

Nassira Nezzar

i Fly
because I Can
... said the Dreamer to the world.
www.iamjustbill.com

100

Michelle
Joan
Barulich

Joan has been writing since I was 16 yrs of age. She enjoys writing poetry and songs. Joan is currently studying the Alternative Medicine to comfort and heal people. She says that she has 2 rescued pigeons that have brought me a lot of love and fun for me. She also like learning about house plants and is a big fan on Nikola Tesla. Her hobbies include art, sewing and wood burning and inventing.

Thank you to Inner child press for letting people express there poetry in a peaceful way.

Web link: https://www.facebook.com/michelle.barulich

That's what I like about Tomorrow

Winter clouds fill the sky
High with hopes
And twinkling stars
A promise for tomorrow
That snow will fall
And make a child see the first of a snow fall
That's what I like about tomorrow
They always come along the way
Where dreams can be made
And broken hearts mend
That's what I like about tomorrow
When its time for spring to arrive
New and fresh
Everyday gets closer
With the promise of new flowers
That will fill the warm summer air
And all the colors that come out
Like our imagination
A new hope
For love to grow
A new way of understanding
To find the true essence
What our Creator has in mind for you and me
Just think what tomorrow may bring
A new awakening that will set us all free....

Cold

I walk down this lonely road
And the grounds pavement hits me too hard
Because without your love
I can't seem to go on
Cause its cold
Without you
While the world keeps turning around
It keeps spinning too fast for me
Cold without you
While the rain keeps coming around
And turns of the seasons bring me down
Well, lately I've been pulling down the shades for my
privacy
I couldn't feel the warmth
Projecting onto me
And I remember when life was filled with intimacy
Now its cold
Cause without your love
Is there reason to go on
When its cold
Without your love....

Love is the Word

See no diamonds in the sky
We all wanted to understand why
Pick up the pieces and begin again
Realizing the mistakes we have made
Why must we try and then lose the nerve
Searching for the way into my heart
But ignoring the word that makes the start
Love is the word that should be heard
From coast to coast and around the world
All around the world
The people's faces are so sad
All around the world
The countries are so mad
That's why this poem is going to make you scream and
shout
Love is the word that should be heard
From coast to coast and around the world
I hope they hear are message
They soon will take
No more nothing if they push the button
No more time to reconsider
Love is the world that should be heard
From coast to coast and around the world
Everybody, Love is the world that should be heard
From coast to coast and around the world....

Monsif Beroual

Monsif Beroual was born in Rabat, Morocco, on October 19th, 1994. He is studying his fourth year of Law Degree at the Sidi Mohammed Ben Adlallah University in Taza, Morocco. Multi awarded poet fom Morocco, winner of the prize - Neruda medal award 2017. Recipient of the Pentasi B. World International Poetry Award in Africa, Ghana 2016 and Pentasi B. World Hyderabad Poetry Award, India 2017.

Director of Morocco at the International Writers Capital Literature Foundation established in India. He has been appointed Director of Youth in Morocco. His poems have been translated into Spanish, French and Arabic; read on radio programs in: Canada, Chiacago, Argentina and Mexico. They have been published in different international journals and anthologies.

My Holly Muse

Our life is like a song
Writing by gold
In every word
Filled of joy
We are in love
Like spring's season
Fully of beauty.
She is my muse
The ink of love fills my heart
Word after word
Made by gold
Carried by wind
Whispers in my ears
Rock my heart
Shaking my soul
Burns, burns, with the fire of love
Burning us
Dancing under the moon's light
Reaching the skies
The seven skies
There's no limit
For our love
Is infinity love
As the space and time
Endless
Cause she is
My holly muse
My living poem
And my heaven gift.

Refugee

Bring me back to my town
where I belong
I missed all
my friends
my childhood
and all the walls.
It was so wonderful
and now all is destroyed
like it never was
my town
my town
my town
I try to scream so loud
but no one hears
my tears.

I still have just the memories
from the past lives on my mind
my stories with my neighbors are gone
and every innocent kid
their dreams were raped
children dies
and history like never exits.
I'm just a number now
without identity
like a dead man
counting the stars in the sky
waiting the consciences
to hear their cries
and their pains
to hold them again
and lead them to their town.

Mirror Of Hope

Woke up this morning
With the voice's whispers in my ears
Led me to that mirror
I saw humans
Brothers and sisters
I saw the wars everywhere
I saw the strong eating the weak
I saw friend betrays his friends
And I saw racism still stand tall between us
Terrorists menacing everywhere
Where is the bright future for us?
I'm not the messenger
I'm not an angel
I'm not perfect
I'm just a human who feels the taste of defeat
Tries to change the situation through that faint
voice
I look like a blind who walks in daylight
Policy made us enemies
And we forgot
We are from one race
Humans, brothers and sisters
I wonder where did the white dove gone!

Krystyna Konecka

Krystyna Konecka is a poet and journalist (a member of The Polish Writers' Union - Warsaw branch). In poetry she favours sonnets. She is an author of nearly twenty books of poetry and reportages. Her poems have been published in Polish and foreign periodicals and anthologies. For her achievements poetry and journalism Krystyna Konecka has received literary awards and was highly regarded by critics. She attends the international literary meetings.

Reading Petrarch's 211 Sonnet To Laura

Year one thousand three hundred twenty-seven.
Sixth day of April, in the morning hour.
I entered the maze which I still have not left.
                    Francesco Petrarca

Year one thousand three hundred twenty-seven.
Six day of April, in the morning hour.
You entered the maze which you have not yet left
though seven ages pass with Tiber waters.

Six hundred and sixty-six of Aprils passed.
Law of coincidence. Me at Capitol
where Rome bowed to you at the centenaries
and placed the wreath of laurels on your temple.

Through chaos of the world in madmen's power
I attempt to save my order by sonnet
by climbing up your path full of the rigours.

You understand, Master – it's not about wreaths.
The wise criticize me. But unluckily
- I entered the maze. I still cannot get out.

Translated by Ewa Sherman, England

Silence. VI

Each step is important as it is dangerous.
Each word becomes essential for the appropriate code.
I fail to hit nail on the head and it will sound false.
I use wrongly and it will be a double edged sword.

We stand facing each other without a word. No shouts.
And every so often we are on the same wavelength.
We smile respectfully to someone from a distance
before they begin to speak in a different language.

We declare that we are the alpha and omega.
Indispensable support and ultimate brink
consolation as well as a mouthful of fresh air.

Yet fear is within us. And we bury our heads
in our arms knowing truly that we were given
no stabilization. Nothing is everlasting.

Translated by Ewa Sherman, England

Ultima Thule. Voices Of Iceland There

From the continent's comforts forgotten for a while.
From the landscapes full of blooms and the soaring forests
of
- trusting the magical power – behind the curve
fortune I fall into Icelandic time reversal.
This stunning madness of rock formations appearing
from all sides. Glittering glacier from the horizon.
By the lava edge a sign banning herding of rams
and sheep warns against perils on the gravel highway.
Yet, on the other hands, us – the creatures with two legs –
in a tenacious four-wheel drive car we take the risk.
To touch with our own eyes the menacing expanse.
Just for the sake of climbing up towards the crater.
  Let it burn with seething saga of those still eras.
  Let it kindle with thirst for fire. Before we fade…

Translated by Ewa Sherman, England

Nassira Nezzar

Nassira Nezzar, A writer from Guelma –Algeria- She was an English language teacher at the university of May 8[th]1945 Guelma for 8 years and a teacher in a National institute for vocational training...She adores writing since young age...Nassira Nezzar has a published book, "FAMILIAR STRANGERS, a collaboration work with the American author Rob McBride, She has collaborative poems with the American author John E WordSlinger, they are available on youtube .

Nassira Nezzar has also many participations in international anthologies which were published in USA, Poland, India, Belgium...

Her website is: http://www.wordsocean.wordpress.com

Sometimes a word

Have you ever contemplated the poet's eyes?
And how they hold the huge mass of words
Have you ever seen the rebellion of stars in the skies
And how they hold each other for brightening our world?
Have you ever stared at the trip of words
And how they delve deeply
into hearts despite the long miles?
Sometimes a word
Hugs our dreams to irrigate them with joy
Sometimes a word
Hugs our reality to throw us as if we're a used toy..
Sometimes a word
Takes me to the depth of your world
Where there's no hate, no discrimination, no wars
No jealousy, no oppression, and no difference of religions
Yes...your world...
Where I see only the eyes of a loving poet
A poet...
Who lives the storms but spreads tranquillity
Who collects words of love and joy to forget his misery
Who collects his tears and his smiles
 For being an ocean of words that could carry
 the feeling with its various weights and sizes
Three drops were following each other without stop

The Farthest I've Gone

Three drops were following each other
The first said: THE FARTHEST
The second said: l 'VE GONE
The third said: WITH YOU
THE FARTHEST I'VE GONE WITH YOU
My ears were fixed on the sound made by your heartbeats.
My eyes were fixed on the pride built on your eyelids
My feeling climbed with blissful heights of love
Looking above..
Searching the pinnacle of your heart..
The farthest I've gone with you
Your love delved into my soul deeply
You were whispering:
I'm the joy that covers your sadness
I'm the peace that covers your frightfulness
I'm the small embrace in which you find vastness
I'm you and the farthest you've gone to my heart
You'll discover many things and « ME »
The farthest I've gone with you had shown me things
 I can't construe
The farthest I've gone with you the sweetest bridge
I've walked through
The farthest I've gone with you I would like to redo it
 and start new
The farthest I've gone with you time flies in it by fast
We lived the moment without care
of the future or the past
Yes sometimes a word to appear with confidence
Sometimes a word to disguise as the weak flies
So behind the silence they hide
Sometimes a word is said
To feed heart and head

Many smiles may be drawn
And many tears may be shed
Sometimes a word said
Many emotions with great passion they are led
Sometime a word carries many questions
Awaitening one sufficient answer
We are created in this world
For loving each other not for killing or
Using our words as swords

Technology

You're there
Wearing so beautiful dress
Making a seducing gestures
And dancing on nice melodies
They call you the great technology
you look to others
As an eternal prosperity
They all want staying in you
But as one soul not two
No one can judge you because
For all you are too sacred and wonderful..
You are the science of profession
But you are not the perfection
 I'm here to make a pause with you
But not to blame or ask you
To lose your principles
You're so awesome angel
Who penetrated our being
 and brightened our lives
We love you when you are wise
But not when you use
the mask of science to disguise
When you become crazy
 and attract others to you
Did you think one day
That you are the slow death of humanity
By your attempts to transfer human to digital
Yes, you look so incredible
Everything in your world is possible
With your velocity you win time
But you paralyse our minds at same time
Yes technology, you make the world a small village

But because of you
We melt in your digital cage
Forgetting the human embrace
Since you make between us a big space
Despite we are living in the same place
Our hearts adore the screens,
 Neglect the real union
And living the real scenes

Inner Child Press

News

We are so excited to announce the New and upcoming books of some of our Poetry Posse authors.

On the following pages we present to you ...

Jackie Davis Allen

Gail Weston Shazor

hülya n. yılmaz

Nizar Sartawi

Faleeha Hassan

Caroline 'Ceri' Nazareno

William S. Peters, Sr.

Coming January of 2019

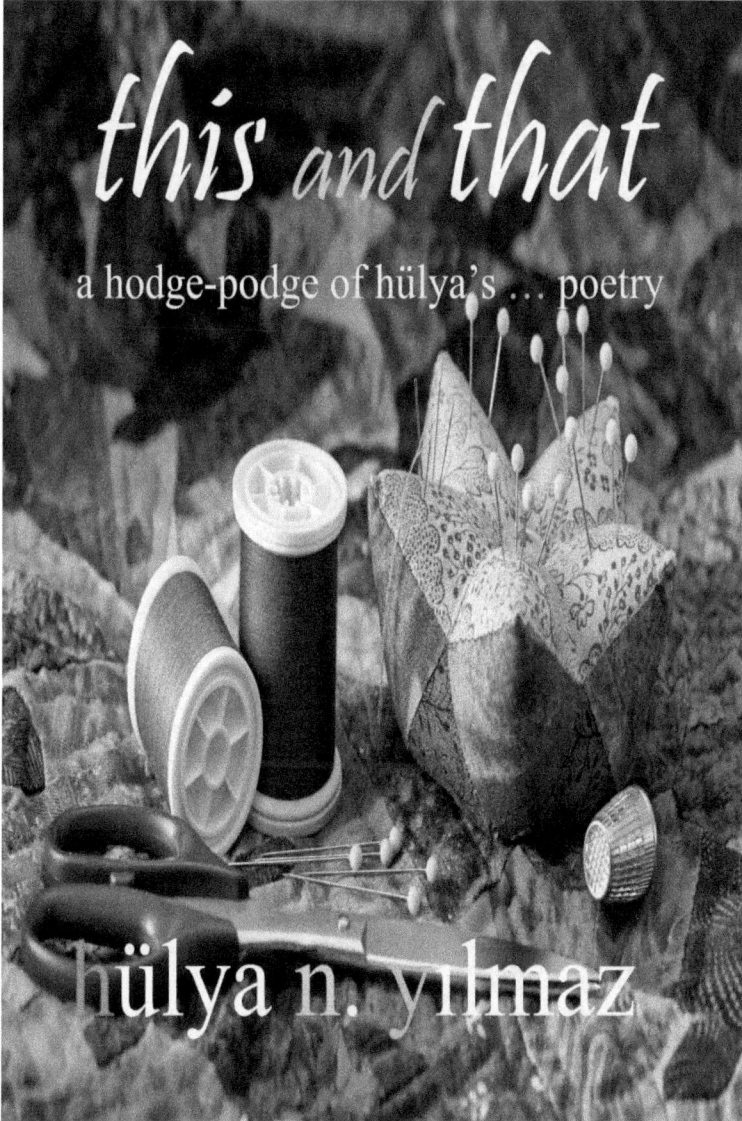

this and that

a hodge-podge of hülya's ... poetry

hülya n. yılmaz

Now Available at
www.innerchildpress.com

Dark Side
of the
Moon

Jackie Davis Allen

Now Available at
www.innerchildpress.com

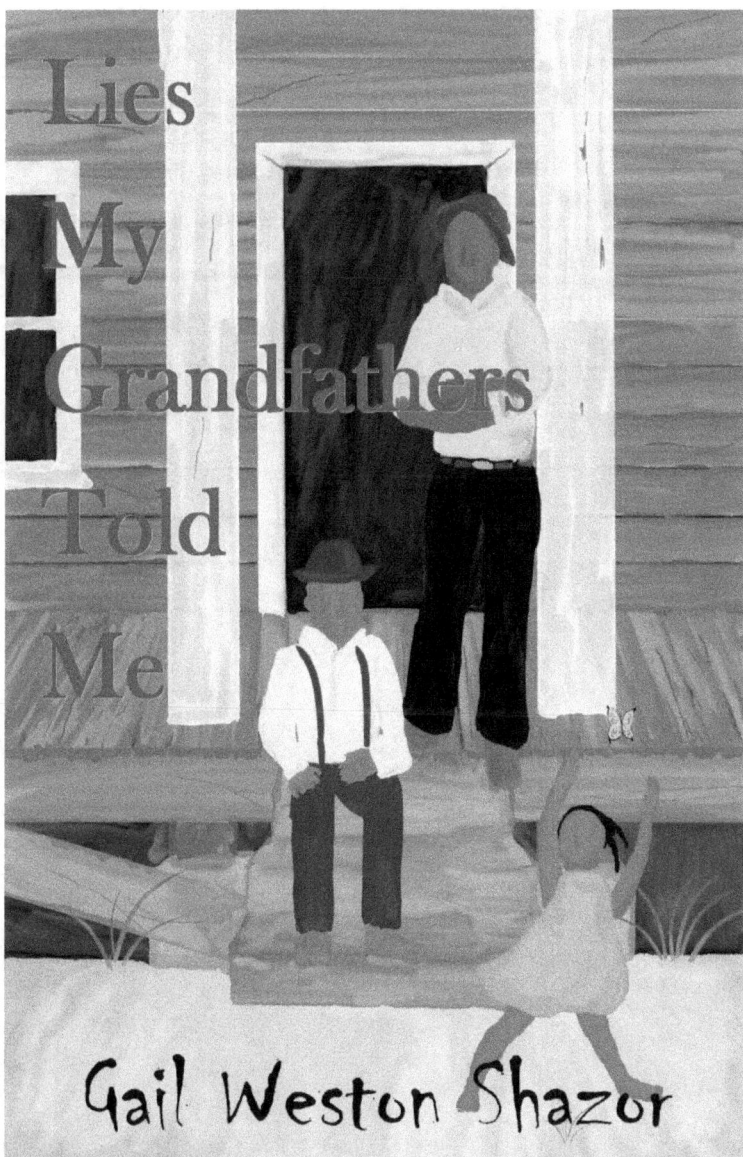

Lies My Grandfathers Told Me

Gail Weston Shazor

Aflame

Memoirs in Verse

hülya n. yılmaz

Now Available at
www.innerchildpress.com

My Shadow

Nizar Sartawi

Now Available at
www.innerchildpress.com

Now Available at
www.innerchildpress.com

Breakfast

for

Butterflies

Faleeha Hassan

Now Available at
www.innerchildpress.com

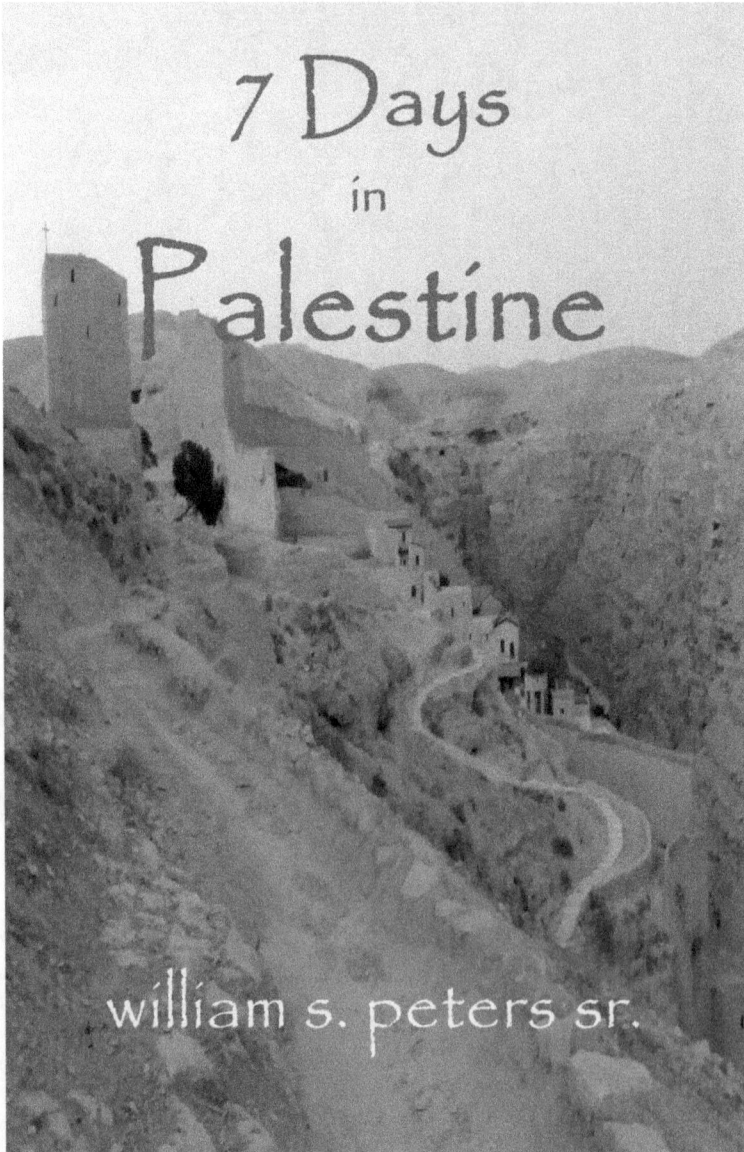

7 Days
in
Palestine

william s. peters sr.

Now Available at
www.innerchildpress.com

inner child press
presents

Tunisia My Love

william s. peters, sr.

Coming in December of 2018

The Journey

Footprints and Shadows

Kosovo

Tunisia

Macedonia

Morocco

Jordan

Palestine

Israel

Italy

Turkey

a collection of poetry inspired during my travels

william s. peters, sr.

Now Available at
www.innerchildpress.com

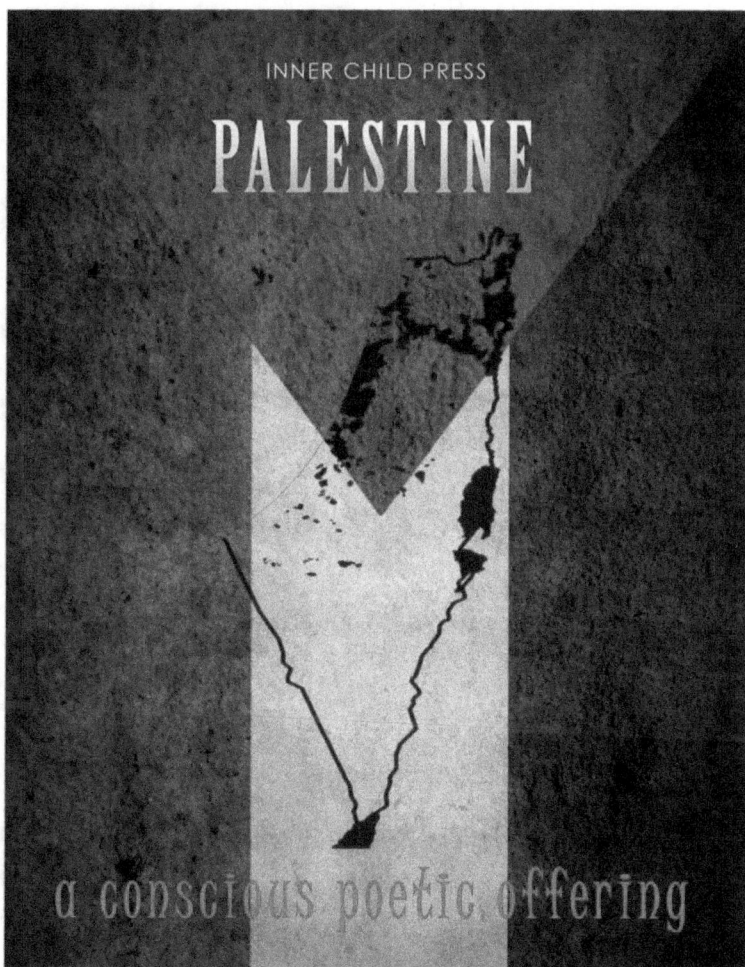

INNER CHILD PRESS

PALESTINE

a conscious poetic offering

Now Available at
www.innerchildpress.com

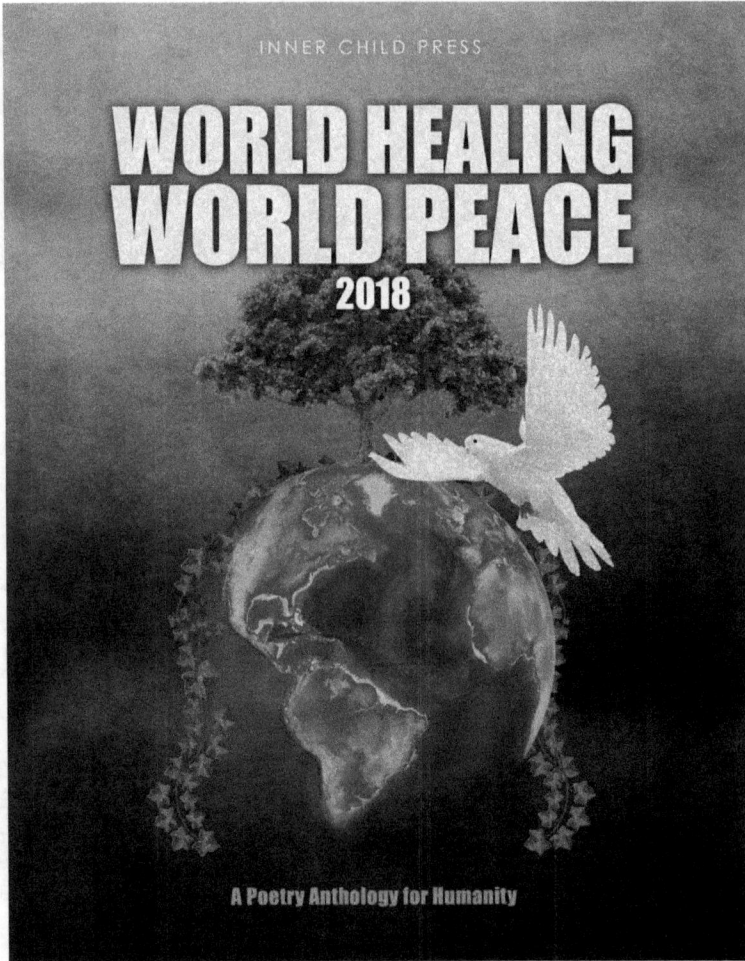

INNER CHILD PRESS

WORLD HEALING
WORLD PEACE
2018

A Poetry Anthology for Humanity

Now Available at
www.innerchildpress.com

INNER CHILD PRESS

THIS IS WHY I
SLEEP

william s. peters sr.

Now Available at
www.innerchildpress.com

Inward Reflections

Think on These Things
Book II

william s. peters, sr.

Now Available at
www.innerchildpress.com

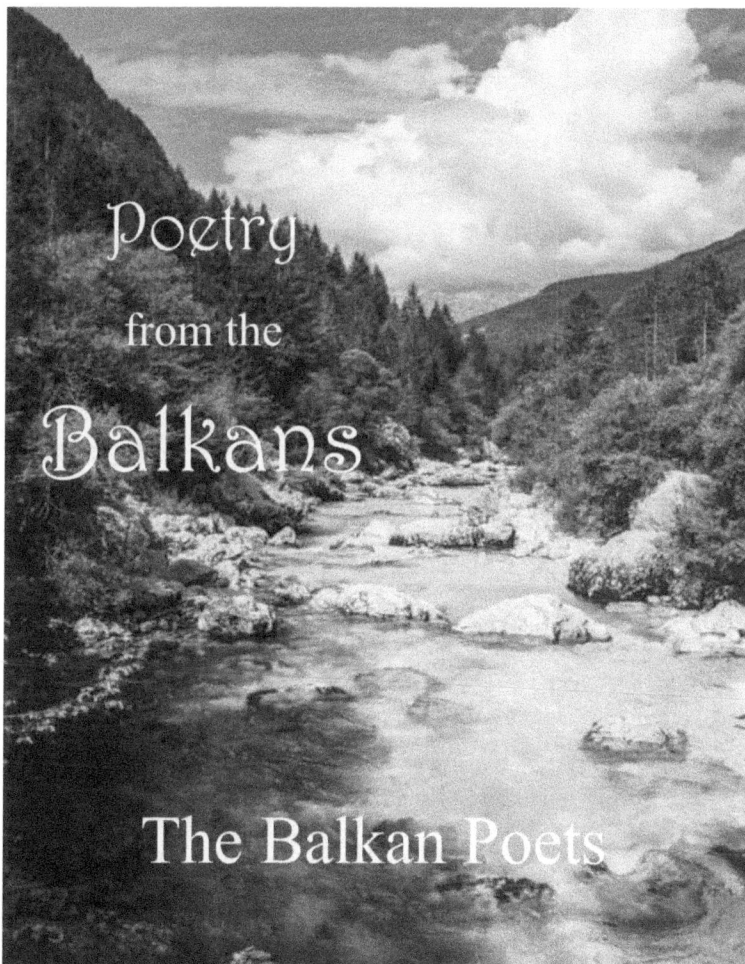

Poetry
from the
Balkans

The Balkan Poets

Other

Anthological

works from

Inner Child Press, ltd.

www.innerchildpress.com

Now Available

www.innerchildpress.com/janet-p-caldwell.php

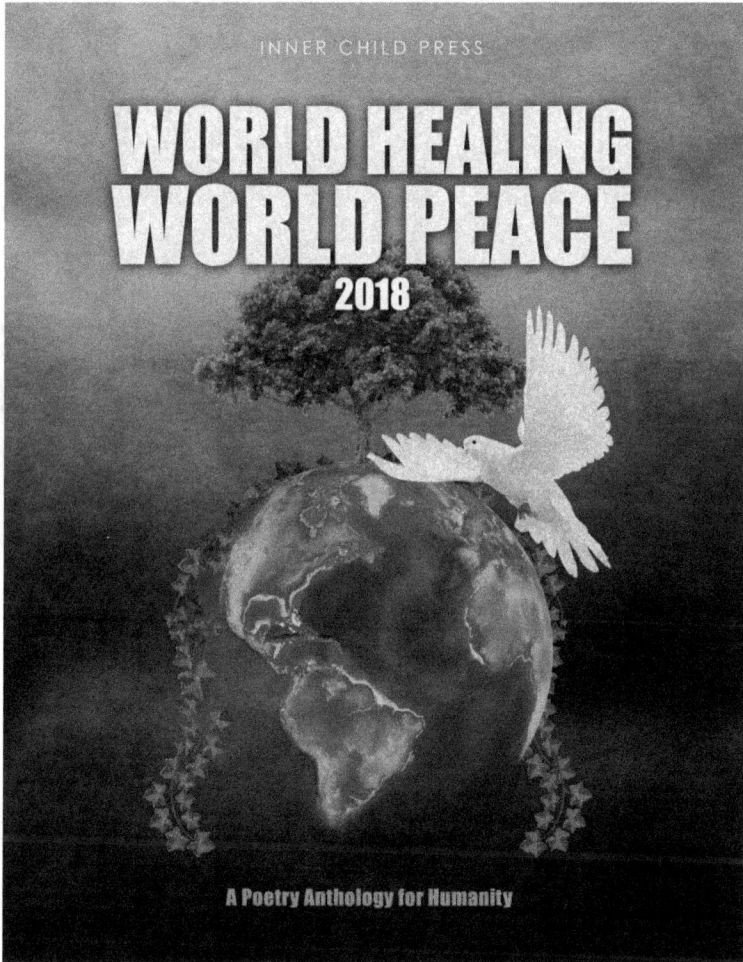

INNER CHILD PRESS

WORLD HEALING WORLD PEACE
2018

A Poetry Anthology for Humanity

Now Available

www.worldhealingworldpeacepoetry.com

Now Available

www.worldhealingworldpeacepoetry.com

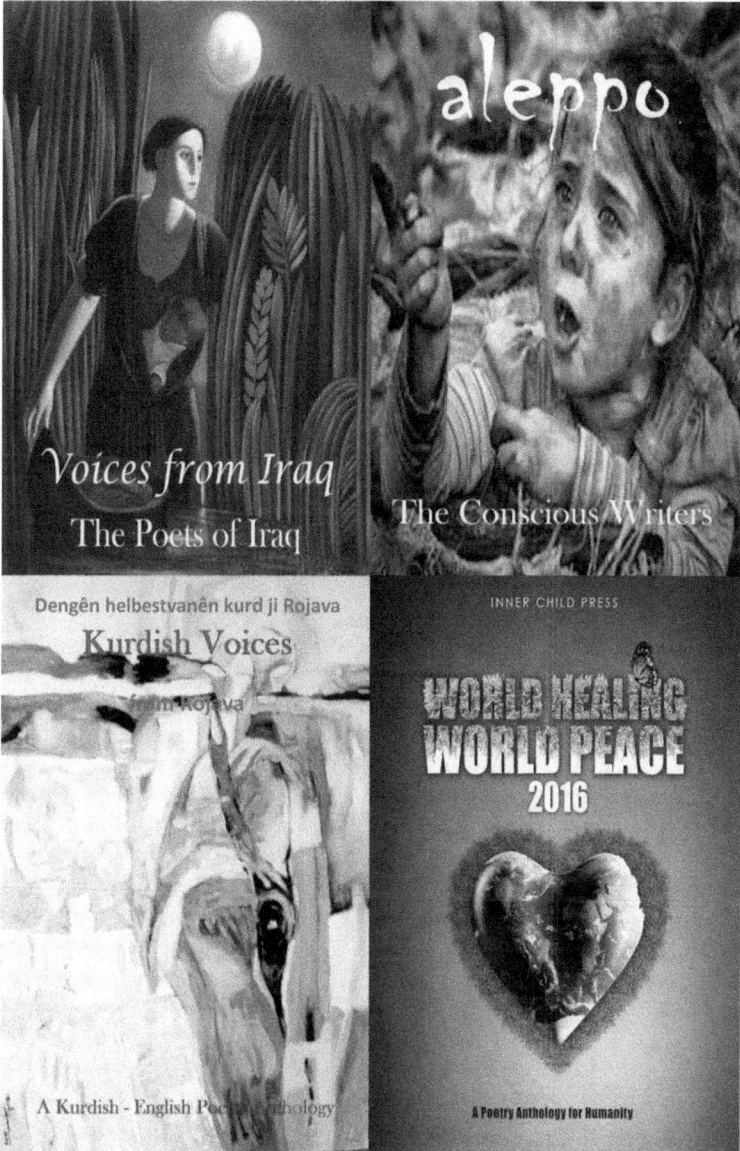

Now Available

www.innerchildpress.com/anthologies

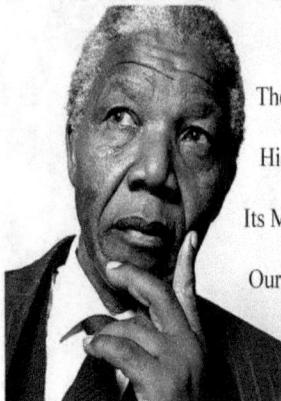

Mandela

The Man

His Life

Its Meaning

Our Words

Poetry . . . Commentary & Stories
The Anthological Writers

A GATHERING OF WORDS

POETRY & COMMENTARY
FOR
TRAYVON MARTIN

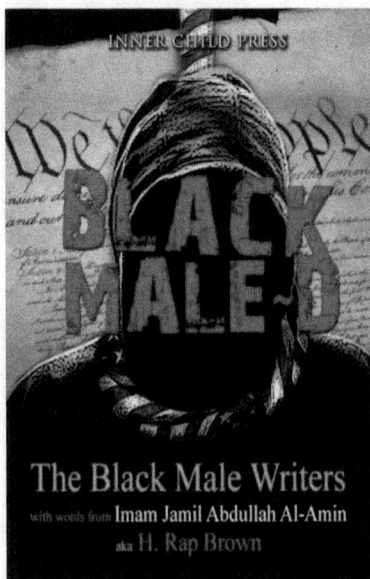

INNER CHILD PRESS

BLACK MALE~D

The Black Male Writers
with words from Imam Jamil Abdullah Al-Amin
aka H. Rap Brown

Now Available

www.innerchildpress.com/anthologies

Now Available

Poetry ... Prose ... Prayer ... Stories

a
Poetically
Spoken
Anthology
volume 1
Collector's Edition

The Poetry Posse
Presents

an anthology
of

Love

The Poetry Posse 2016

Now Available

www.innerchildpress.com/anthologies

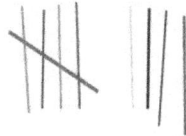

Now Available

www.innerchildpress.com/anthologies

The Year of the Poet
January 2014

The Poetry Posse

Jamie Bond
Gail Weston Shazor
Albert 'Infinite' Carrasco
Siddartha Beth Pierce
Janet P. Caldwell
June 'Bugg' Barefield
Debbie M. Allen
Tony Henninger
Joe DaVerbal Minddancer
Robert Gibbons
Neetu Wali
Shareef Abdur-Rasheed
William S. Peters, Sr.

Carnation

Our January Feature
Terri L. Johnson

the Year of the Poet
February 2014

violets

The Poetry Posse

Jamie Bond
Gail Weston Shazor
Albert 'Infinite' Carrasco
Siddartha Beth Pierce
Janet P. Caldwell
June 'Bugg' Barefield
Debbie M. Allen
Tony Henninger
Joe DaVerbal Minddancer
Robert Gibbons
Neetu Wali
Shareef Abdur-Rasheed
William S. Peters, Sr.

Our February Features
Teresa E. Gallion & Robert Gibson

The Year of the Poet
March 2014

The Poetry Posse

Jamie Bond
Gail Weston Shazor
Albert 'Infinite' Carrasco
Siddartha Beth Pierce
Janet P. Caldwell
June 'Bugg' Barefield
Debbie M. Allen
Tony Henninger
Joe DaVerbal Minddancer
Robert Gibbons
Neetu Wali
Shareef Abdur-Rasheed
Kimberly Burnham
William S. Peters, Sr.

daffodil

Our March Featured Poets
Alicia C. Cooper & hülya yılmaz

the Year of the Poet
April 2014

The Poetry Posse

Jamie Bond
Gail Weston Shazor
Albert 'Infinite' Carrasco
Siddartha Beth Pierce
Janet P. Caldwell
June 'Bugg' Barefield
Debbie M. Allen
Tony Henninger
Joe DaVerbal Minddancer
Robert Gibbons
Neetu Wali
Shareef Abdur-Rasheed
Kimberly Burnham
William S. Peters, Sr.

Our April Featured Poets
Fahredin Shehu
Martina Reisz Newberry
Justin Blackburn
Monte Smith

Sweet Pea

celebrating international poetry month

Now Available

www.innerchildpress.com/the-year-of-the-poet

154

Now Available

The Year of the Poet
September 2014

Aster   Morning-Glory

Wild Columbine September Birth Flower

September Feature Poets
Florence Malone • Keith Alan Hamilton

The Poetry Posse
Jamie Bond • Gail Weston Shazor • Albert 'Infinite' Carrasco • Siddartha Beth Pierce
Janet P. Caldwell • June 'Bugg' Barefield • Debbie M. Allen • Tony Henninger
Joe DaVerbal Minddancer • Robert Gibbons • Neetu Wali • Shareef Abdur-Rasheed
Kimberly Burnham • William S. Peters, Sr.

THE YEAR OF THE POET
October 2014

Red Poppy

The Poetry Posse
Jamie Bond • Gail Weston Shazor • Albert 'Infinite' Carrasco • Siddartha Beth Pierce
Janet P. Caldwell • June 'Bugg' Barefield • Debbie M. Allen • Tony Henninger
Joe DaVerbal Minddancer • Robert Gibbons • Neetu Wali • Shareef Abdur-Rasheed
Kimberly Burnham • William S. Peters, Sr.

October Feature Poets
Ceri Naz • Rajendra Padhi • Elizabeth Castillo

THE YEAR OF THE POET
November 2014

Chrysanthemum

The Poetry Posse

November Feature Poets
Jocelyn Mosman • Jackie Allen • James Moore • Neville Hiatt

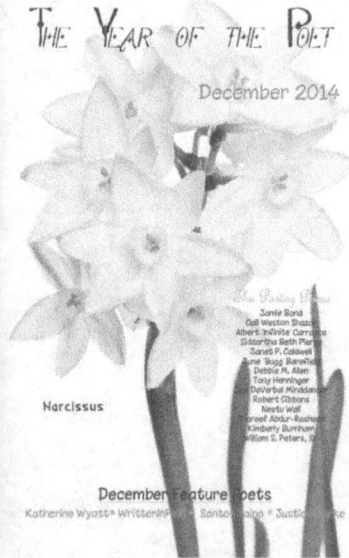

THE YEAR OF THE POET
December 2014

Narcissus

December Feature Poets
Katherine Wyatt • Writtenink • Santosh Bajan • Justin Burke

Now Available

www.innerchildpress.com/the-year-of-the-poet

156

THE YEAR OF THE POET II

January 2015

Garnet

The Poetry Posse

Jamie Bond
Gail Weston Shazor
Albert 'Infinite' Carrasco
Siddartha Beth Pierce
Janet P. Caldwell
Tony Henninger
Joe DaVerbal Minddancer
Robert Gibbons
Neetu Wali
Shareef Abdur – Rasheed
Kimberly Burnham
Ann White
Keith Alan Hamilton
Katherine Wyatt
Fahredin Shehu
Hülya N. Yılmaz
Teresa E. Gallion
Jackie Allen
William S. Peters, Sr.

January Feature Poets

Bismay Mohanti * Jen Walls * Eric Judah

THE YEAR OF THE POET II

February 2015

Amethyst

THE POETRY POSSE

Jamie Bond
Gail Weston Shazor
Albert 'Infinite' Carrasco
Siddartha Beth Pierce
Janet P. Caldwell
Tony Henninger
Joe DaVerbal Minddancer
Robert Gibbons
Neetu Wali
Shareef Abdur – Rasheed
Kimberly Burnham
Ann White
Keith Alan Hamilton
Katherine Wyatt
Hülya N. Yılmaz
Teresa E. Gallion
Jackie Allen
William S. Peters, Sr.

FEBRUARY FEATURE POETS

Iram Fatima * Bob McNeil * Kerstin Centervall

The Year of the Poet II

March 2015

Our Featured Poets

Heung Sook * Anthony Arnold * Alicia Poland

Bloodstone

The Poetry Posse 2015

Jamie Bond * Gail Weston Shazor * Albert 'Infinite' Carrasco
Siddartha Beth Pierce * Janet P. Caldwell * Tony Henninger
Joe DaVerbal Minddancer * Neetu Wali * Shareef Abdur – Rasheed
Kimberly Burnham * Ann White * Keith Alan Hamilton
Katherine Wyatt * Fahredin Shehu * Hülya N. Yılmaz
Teresa E. Gallion * Jackie Allen * William S. Peters, Sr.

The Year of the Poet II

April 2015

Celebrating International Poetry Month

Our Featured Poets

Raja Williams * Dennis Ferado * Laure Charazac

Diamonds

The Poetry Posse 2015

Jamie Bond * Gail Weston Shazor * Albert 'Infinite' Carrasco
Siddartha Beth Pierce * Janet P. Caldwell * Tony Henninger
Joe DaVerbal Minddancer * Neetu Wali * Shareef Abdur – Rasheed
Kimberly Burnham * Ann White * Keith Alan Hamilton
Katherine Wyatt * Fahredin Shehu * Hülya N. Yılmaz
Teresa E. Gallion * Jackie Allen * William S. Peters, Sr.

Now Available

www.innerchildpress.com/the-year-of-the-poet

The Year of the Poet II
May 2015

May's Featured Poets
Geri Algeri
Akin Mosi Chinners
Anna Jakubcza

Emeralds

The Poetry Posse 2015
Jamie Bond * Gail Weston Shazor * Albert 'Infinite' Carrasco
Siddartha Beth Pierce * Janet P. Caldwell * Tony Henninger
Joe DaVerbal Minddancer * Neetu Wali * Shareef Abdur - Rasheed
Kimberly Burnham * Ann White * Keith Alan Hamilton
Katherine Wyatt * Fahredin Shehu * Hülya N. Yılmaz
Teresa E. Gallion * Jackie Allen * William S. Peters, Sr.

The Year of the Poet II
June 2015

June's Featured Poets
Anahit Arustamyan * Yvette D. Murrell * Regina A. Walker

Pearl

The Poetry Posse 2015
Jamie Bond * Gail Weston Shazor * Albert 'Infinite' Carrasco
Siddartha Beth Pierce * Janet P. Caldwell * Tony Henninger
Joe DaVerbal Minddancer * Neetu Wali * Shareef Abdur - Rasheed
Kimberly Burnham * Ann White * Keith Alan Hamilton
Katherine Wyatt * Fahredin Shehu * Hülya N. Yılmaz
Teresa E. Gallion * Jackie Allen * William S. Peters, Sr

The Year of the Poet II
July 2015

The Featured Poets for July 2015
Abhik Shome * Christina Neal * Robert Neal

Rubies

The Poetry Posse 2015
Jamie Bond * Gail Weston Shazor * Albert 'Infinite' Carrasco
Siddartha Beth Pierce * Janet P. Caldwell * Tony Henninger
Joe DaVerbal Minddancer * Neetu Wali * Shareef Abdur - Rasheed
Kimberly Burnham * Ann White * Keith Alan Hamilton
Katherine Wyatt * Fahredin Shehu * Hülya N. Yılmaz
Teresa E. Gallion * Jackie Allen * William S. Peters, Sr.

The Year of the Poet II
August 2015

Peridot

Featured Poets
Gayle Howell
Ann Chalasz
Christopher Schultz

The Poetry Posse 2015
Jamie Bond * Gail Weston Shazor * Albert 'Infinite' Carrasco
Siddartha Beth Pierce * Janet P. Caldwell * Tony Henninger
Joe DaVerbal Minddancer * Neetu Wali * Shareef Abdur - Rasheed
Kimberly Burnham * Ann White * Keith Alan Hamilton
Katherine Wyatt * Fahredin Shehu * Hülya N. Yılmaz
Teresa E. Gallion * Jackie Allen * William S. Peters, Sr.

Now Available

www.innerchildpress.com/the-year-of-the-poet

The Year of the Poet II
September 2015

Featured Poets
Alfreda Ghee / Lonneice Weeks Badley / Demetrios Trifiatis

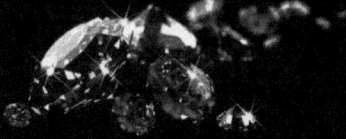

Sapphires

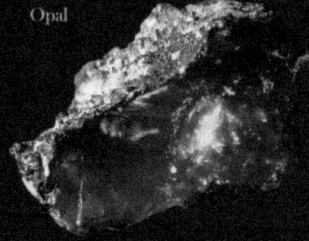

The Poetry Posse 2015
Jamie Bond * Gail Weston Shazor * Albert 'Infinite' Carrasco
Siddartha Beth Pierce * Janet P. Caldwell * Tony Henninger
Joe DaVerbal Minddancer * Neetu Wali * Shareef Abdur – Rasheed
Kimberly Burnham * Ann White * Keith Alan Hamilton
Katherine Wyatt * Fahredin Shehu * Hülya N. Yılmaz
Teresa E. Gallion * Jackie Allen * William S. Peters, Sr.

The Year of the Poet II
October 2015

Featured Poets
Monte Smith * Laura J. Wolfe * William Washington

Opal

The Poetry Posse 2015
Jamie Bond * Gail Weston Shazor * Albert 'Infinite' Carrasco
Siddartha Beth Pierce * Janet P. Caldwell * Tony Henninger
Joe DaVerbal Minddancer * Neetu Wali * Shareef Abdur – Rasheed
Kimberly Burnham * Ann White * Keith Alan Hamilton
Katherine Wyatt * Fahredin Shehu * Hülya N. Yılmaz
Teresa E. Gallion * Jackie Allen * William S. Peters, Sr.

The Year of the Poet II
November 2015

Featured Poets
Alan W. Jankowski
Bisnay Mohanty
James Moore

Topaz

The Poetry Posse 2015
Jamie Bond * Gail Weston Shazor * Albert 'Infinite' Carrasco
Siddartha Beth Pierce * Janet P. Caldwell * Tony Henninger
Joe DaVerbal Minddancer * Neetu Wali * Shareef Abdur – Rasheed
Kimberly Burnham * Ann White * Keith Alan Hamilton
Katherine Wyatt * Fahredin Shehu * Hülya N. Yılmaz
Teresa E. Gallion * Jackie Allen * William S. Peters, Sr.

The Year of the Poet II
December 2015

Featured Poets
Kerione Bryan * Michelle Joan Barulich * Neville Hiatt

Turquoise

The Poetry Posse 2015
Jamie Bond * Gail Weston Shazor * Albert 'Infinite' Carrasco
Siddartha Beth Pierce * Janet P. Caldwell * Tony Henninger
Joe DaVerbal Minddancer * Neetu Wali * Shareef Abdur – Rasheed
Kimberly Burnham * Ann White * Keith Alan Hamilton
Katherine Wyatt * Fahredin Shehu * Hülya N. Yılmaz
Teresa E. Gallion * Jackie Allen * William S. Peters, Sr.

Now Available

www.innerchildpress.com/the-year-of-the-poet

The Year of the Poet III
January 2016

Featured Poets

Lana Joseph * Atom Cyrus Rush * Christena Williams

Dark-eyed Junco

The Poetry Posse 2016

Gail Weston Shazor * Anna Jakubczak * Val Batty Valdez * Ann J. White
Fahredin Shehu * Mbizabush Padnya * Janet P. Caldwell
Joe DaVerbal Minddancer * Sharout Abdur - Rasheed
Albert Carrasco * Kimberly Burnham * Keith Alan Hamilton
Hülya N. Yılmaz * Demetrios Trifiatis * Alan W. Jankowski
Teresa E. Gallion * Jackie Davis Allen * William S. Peters, Sr.

The Year of the Poet III
February 2016

Featured Poets

Anthony Arnold
Anna Chalasz
Dr. Andre Hawthorne

Puffin

The Poetry Posse 2016

Gail Weston Shazor * Joe DaVerbal Minddancer * Alfredo Ghee
Fahredin Shehu * Hirshhdesh Padnya * Janet P. Caldwell
Anna Jakubczak Val Batty Valdez * Sharout Abdur - Rasheed
Albert Carrasco * Kimberly Burnham * Ann J. White
Hülya N. Yılmaz * Demetrios Trifiatis * Alan W. Jankowski
Teresa E. Gallion * Jackie Davis Allen * William S. Peters, Sr.

The Year of the Poet
March 2016

Featured Poets

Jeton Kelmendi   Nizar Sartawi   Sami Muhanna

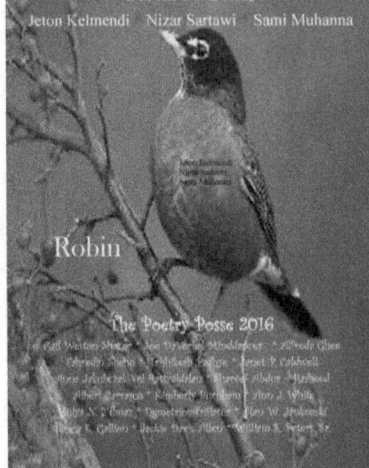

Robin

The Poetry Posse 2016

Gail Weston Shazor * Joe DaVerbal Minddancer * Alfredo Ghee
Fahredin Shehu * Hirshhdesh Padnya * Janet P. Caldwell
Anna Jakubczak Val Batty Valdez * Sharout Abdur - Rasheed
Albert Carrasco * Kimberly Burnham * Ann J. White
Hülya N. Yılmaz * Demetrios Trifiatis * Alan W. Jankowski
Teresa E. Gallion * Jackie Davis Allen * William S. Peters, Sr.

The Year of the Poet III

Featured Poets

Ali Abdolrezaei

Anna Chalasz

Agim Vinca

Ceri Naz

Black Capped Chickadee

The Poetry Posse 2016

Gail Weston Shazor * Joe DaVerbal Minddancer * Alfredo Ghee
Fahredin Shehu * Hirshhdesh Padnya * Janet P. Caldwell
Anna Jakubczak Val Batty Valdez * Sharout Abdur - Rasheed
Albert Carrasco * Kimberly Burnham * Ann J. White
Hülya N. Yılmaz * Demetrios Trifiatis * Alan W. Jankowski
Teresa E. Gallion * Jackie Davis Allen * William S. Peters, Sr.

celebrating international poetry month

Now Available

www.innerchildpress.com/the-year-of-the-poet

The Year of the Poet May 2016

Bob Strum
Barbara Allan
D.L. Davis

Oriole

The Poetry Posse 2016

The Year of the Poet III June 2016

Featured Poets

Qibrije Demiri- Frangu
Naime Beqiraj
Faleeha Hassan
Bedri Zyberaj

Black Necked Stilt

The Poetry Posse 2016

The Year of the Poet III July

Iram Fatima 'Ashi'
Langley Shazor
Jody Doty
Emilia T. Davis

Indigo Bunting

The Poetry Posse 2016

The Year of the Poet III August 2016

Featured Poets

Anita Dash
Irena Jovanovic
Malgorzata Gouluda

Painted Bunting

The Poetry Posse 2016

Now Available

www.innerchildpress.com/the-year-of-the-poet

161

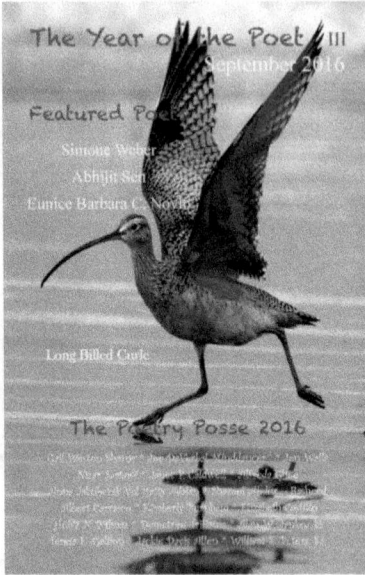

The Year of the Poet III
September 2016

Featured Poets

Simone Weber
Abhijit Sen
Eunice Barbara C. Novio

Long Billed Curle

The Poetry Posse 2016

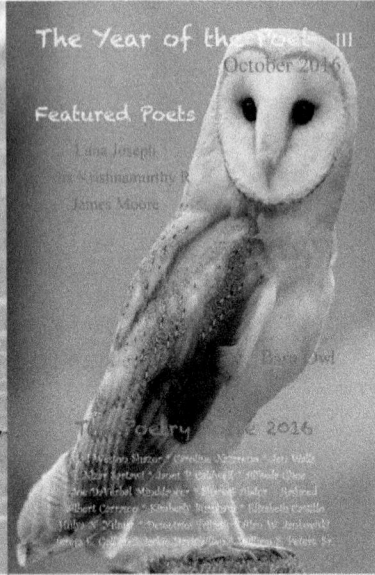

The Year of the Poet III
October 2016

Featured Poets

Lana Joseph
Sri Krishnamurthy R
James Moore

Barn Owl

The Poetry Posse 2016

The Year of the Poet III
November 2016

Featured Poets

Rosemary Burns
Robin Ouzman Hislop
Lonneice Weeks-Badley

Northern Cardinal

The Poetry Posse 2016

Gil Weston Shaver * Caroline Nazareno * Jen Walls
Mize Bottani * Janet P. Caldwell * Alfreda Ghee
Joe DaVerbal Minddancer * Shareef Abdur - Rasheed
Albert Carrasco * Kimberly Burnham * Elizabeth Castillo
Hülya N. Yılmaz * Demetrios Trifiatis * Alan W. Jankowski
Teresa E. Gallion * Jackie Davis Allen * William S. Peters, Sr.

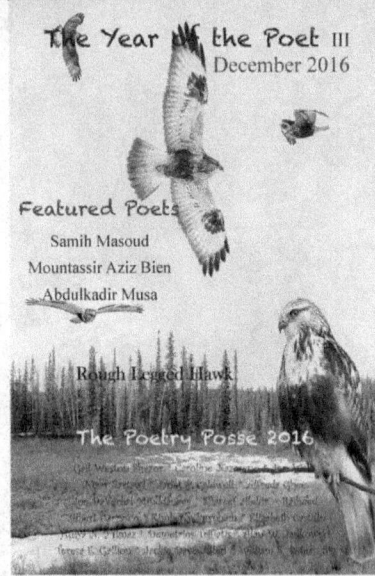

The Year of the Poet III
December 2016

Featured Poets

Samih Masoud
Mountassir Aziz Bien
Abdulkadir Musa

Rough Legged Hawk

The Poetry Posse 2016

Now Available

www.innerchildpress.com/the-year-of-the-poet

The Year of the Poet IV
January 2017

Featured Poets

Jon Winell
Natalie Shields
Irani Fatima "Ashi"

Quaking Aspen

The Poetry Posse 2017

Gail Weston Shazor * Caroline Nazareno * Bismay Mohanty
Niyer Sortawt * Anna Jakubczak Vel Ratty Adalan * Jen Walls
Joe DaVerbal Minddancer * Shareef Abdur - Rasheed
Albert Carrasco * Kimberly Burnham * Elizabeth Castillo
Hülya N. Yılmaz * Teleeha Hassan * Alan W. Jankowski
Teresa E. Gallion * Jackie Davis Allen * William S. Peters, Sr.

The Year of the Poet IV
February 2017

Featured Poets

Lin Ross
Soulaima Fathi
Anwer Gitani

Witch Hazel

The Poetry Posse 2017

Gail Weston Shazor * Caroline Nazareno * Bismay Mohanty
Niyer Sortawt * Anna Jakubczak Vel Ratty Adalan * Jen Walls
Joe DaVerbal Minddancer * Shareef Abdur - Rasheed
Albert Carrasco * Kimberly Burnham * Elizabeth Castillo
Hülya N. Yılmaz * Teleeha Hassan * Alan W. Jankowski
Teresa E. Gallion * Jackie Davis Allen * William S. Peters, Sr.

The Year of the Poet IV
March 2017

Featured Poets

Tremell Stevens
Francisca Richnski
Jamit Abu Shaih

The Eastern Redbud

The Poetry Posse 2017

Gail Weston Shazor * Caroline Nazareno * Bismay Mohanty
Teresa E. Gallion * Anna Jakubczak Vel Ratty Adalan
Joe DaVerbal Minddancer * Shareef Abdur - Rasheed
Albert Carrasco * Kimberly Burnham * Elizabeth Castillo
Hülya N. Yılmaz * Teleeha Hassan * Jackie Davis Allen
Jen Walls * Niyer Sortawt * * William S. Peters, Sr.

The Year of the Poet IV
April 2017

Featured Poets

Dr. Ruchida Barman
Neptune Barman
Masood Khalil

The Blossoming Cherry

The Poetry Posse 2017

Gail Weston Shazor * Caroline Nazareno * Bismay Mohanty
Niyer Sortawt * Anna Jakubczak Vel Ratty Adalan * Jen Walls
Joe DaVerbal Minddancer * Shareef Abdur - Rasheed
Albert Carrasco * Kimberly Burnham * Elizabeth Castillo
Hülya N. Yılmaz * Teleeha Hassan * Jackie Davis Allen
Teresa E. Gallion * Niyer Sortawt * * William S. Peters, Sr.

Now Available

www.innerchildpress.com/the-year-of-the-poet

The Year of the Poet IV
May 2017

The Flowering Dogwood Tree

Featured Poets
Kallisa Powell
Alicja Maria Kuberska
Fethi Sassi

The Poetry Posse 2017

Gail Weston Shazor * Caroline Nazareno * Teresa Mohapy
Teresa E. Gallion * Anna Jakubczak Vel Ratty Adalan
Joe DaVerbal Minddancer * Shareef Abdur – Rasheed
Albert Carrasco * Kimberly Burnham * Elizabeth Castillo
Hülya N. Yılmaz * Fahredin Shehu * Jackie Davis Allen
Jan Wolfe * Nizar Sartawi * * William S. Peters, Sr.

The Year of the Poet IV
June 2017

Featured Poets
Eliza Segiet
Tze-Min Tsai
Abdulla Issa

The Linden Tree

The Poetry Posse 2017

Hülya N. Yılmaz
Jan Wolfe * Nizar Sartawi * William S. Peters, Sr.

The Year of the Poet IV
July 2017

Featured Poets
Anca Mihaela Bruma
Ibaa Ismail
Zvonko Taneski

The Oak Moon

The Poetry Posse 2017

Gail Weston Shazor * Caroline Nazareno * Teresa Mohapy
Teresa E. Gallion * Anna Jakubczak Vel Ratty Adalan
Joe DaVerbal Minddancer * Shareef Abdur – Rasheed
Albert Carrasco * Kimberly Burnham * Elizabeth Castillo
Hülya N. Yılmaz * Fahredin Shehu * Jackie Davis Allen
Jan Wolfe * Nizar Sartawi * * William S. Peters, Sr.

The Year of the Poet IV
August 2017

Featured Poets
Jonathan Aquino
Kitty Hsu
Langley Shazor

The Hazelnut Tree

The Poetry Posse 2017

Gail Weston Shazor * Caroline Nazareno *
Teresa E. Gallion * Anna Jakubczak Vel Ratty Adalan
Joe DaVerbal Minddancer * Shareef Abdur – Rasheed
Albert Carrasco * Kimberly Burnham * Elizabeth Castillo
Hülya N. Yılmaz * Fahredin Shehu * Jackie Davis Allen
Jan Wolfe * Nizar Sartawi * * William S. Peters, Sr.

Now Available

www.innerchildpress.com/the-year-of-the-poet

The Year of the Poet IV
September 2017

Featured Poets

Martina Reisz Newberry
Ameer Nassir
Christine Fulco Neal
Robert Neal

The Elm Tree

The Poetry Posse 2017

Gail Weston Shazor * Caroline Nazareno * Bismay Mohanty
Teresa E. Gallion * Anna Jakubczak Vel Ratty Adalan
Joe DaVerbal Minddancer * Shareef Abdur – Rasheed
Albert Carrasco * Kimberly Burnham * Elizabeth Castillo
Hülya N. Yılmaz * Faleeha Hassan * Jackie Davis Allen
Jen Walls * Nizar Sartawi * * William S. Peters, Sr.

The Year of the Poet IV
October 2017

Featured Poets

Ahmed Abu Saleem
Nedal Al-Qaeim
Sadeddin Shahin

The Black Walnut Tree

The Poetry Posse 2017

Gail Weston Shazor * Caroline Nazareno * Bismay Mohanty
Teresa E. Gallion * Anna Jakubczak Vel Ratty Adalan
Joe DaVerbal Minddancer * Shareef Abdur – Rasheed
Albert Carrasco * Kimberly Burnham * Elizabeth Castillo
Hülya N. Yılmaz * Faleeha Hassan * Jackie Davis Allen
Jen Walls * Nizar Sartawi * * William S. Peters, Sr.

The Year of the Poet IV
November 2017

Featured Poets

Kay Peters
Alfreda D. Ghee
Gabriella Garofalo
Rosemary Cappello

The Tree of Life

The Poetry Posse 2017

Gail Weston Shazor * Caroline Nazareno * Bismay Mohanty
Teresa E. Gallion * Anna Jakubczak Vel Ratty Adalan
Joe DaVerbal Minddancer * Shareef Abdur – Rasheed
Albert Carrasco * Kimberly Burnham * Elizabeth Castillo
Hülya N. Yılmaz * Faleeha Hassan * Jackie Davis Allen
Jen Walls * Nizar Sartawi * William S. Peters, Sr.

The Year of the Poet IV
December 2017

Featured Poets

Justice Clarke
Mariel M. Pabroa
Kiley Brown

The Fig Tree

The Poetry Posse 2017

Gail Weston Shazor * Caroline Nazareno * Bismay Mohanty
Teresa E. Gallion * Anna Jakubczak Vel Ratty Adalan
Joe DaVerbal Minddancer * Shareef Abdur – Rasheed
Albert Carrasco * Kimberly Burnham * Elizabeth Castillo
Hülya N. Yılmaz * Faleeha Hassan * Jackie Davis Allen
Jen Walls * Nizar Sartawi * William S. Peters, Sr.

Now Available

www.innerchildpress.com/the-year-of-the-poet

The Year of the Poet V
January 2018
Featured Poets
Iyad Shamasnah
Yasmeen Hamzeh
Ali Abdolrezaei

Aksum

The Poetry Posse 2018
Gail Weston Shazor * Caroline Nazareno * Tezmin Ition Tsai
Hülya N. Yılmaz * Faleeha Hassan * Jackie Davis Allen
Teresa E. Gallion * Anna Jakubczak Vel Ratty Adalan
Alicja Maria Kuberska * Shareef Abdur – Rasheed
Kimberly Burnham * Elizabeth Castillo
Nizar Sartawi * William S. Peters, Sr.

The Year of the Poet V
February 2018

Sabean

Featured Poets
Muhammad Azram
Anna Szawiracka
Abhilipsa Kuanar
Aanika Aery

The Poetry Posse 2018
Gail Weston Shazor * Caroline Nazareno * Tezmin Ition Tsai
Hülya N. Yılmaz * Faleeha Hassan * Jackie Davis Allen
Teresa E. Gallion * Anna Jakubczak Vel Ratty Adalan
Alicja Maria Kuberska * Shareef Abdur – Rasheed
Kimberly Burnham * Elizabeth Castillo
Nizar Sartawi * William S. Peters, Sr.

The Year of the Poet V
March 2018

Featured Poets
Iram Fatima 'Ashi'
Cassandra Swan
Jaleel Khazaal
Shazia Zaman

Mexico
Cuba

Caribbean
&
Middle America

The Poetry Posse 2018
Gail Weston Shazor * Nizar Sartawi * Hülya N. Yılmaz
Jackie Davis Allen * Caroline 'Ceri' Nazareno
Alicja Maria Kuberska * Teresa E. Gallion
Faleeha Hassan * Shareef Abdur – Rasheed
Kimberly Burnham * Elizabeth Castillo
Tezmin Ition Tsai * William S. Peters, Sr.

The Year of the Poet V
April 2018
Featured Poets

The Nez Perce

The Poetry Posse 2018

Now Available

www.innerchildpress.com/the-year-of-the-poet

The Year of the Poet V
May 2018

Featured Poets

The Sumerians

The Poetry Posse 2018

Gail Weston Shazor * Nizar Sartawi * Hülya N. Yılmaz
Jackie Davis Allen * Caroline 'Ceri' Nazareno
Alicja Maria Kuberska * Teresa E. Gallion
Kimberly Burnham * Shareef Abdur – Rasheed
Faleeha Hassan * Elizabeth Castillo * Swapna Behera
Tezmin Ition Tsai * William S. Peters, Sr.

The Year of the Poet V
June 2018

Featured Poets
Bilall Maliqi * Daim Miftari * Gojko Božović * Sofija Živković

The Paleo Indians

The Poetry Posse 2018

The Year of the Poet V
July 2018

Featured Poets

Oceania

The Poetry Posse 2018

The Year of the Poet V
August 2018

Featured Poets
Hussein Habasch * Mircea Dan Duta * Naida Mujkić * Swagat Das

The Lapita

The Poetry Posse 2018

Gail Weston Shazor * Nizar Sartawi * Hülya N. Yılmaz
Jackie Davis Allen * Caroline 'Ceri' Nazareno
Alicja Maria Kuberska * Teresa E. Gallion
Kimberly Burnham * Shareef Abdur – Rasheed
Ashok K. Bhargava * Elizabeth Castillo * Swapna Behaera
Tezmin Ition Tsai * William S. Peters, Sr.

Now Available

www.innerchildpress.com/the-year-of-the-poet

The Year of the Poet V
September 2018

The Aztecs & Incas

Featured Poets
Kolade Olanrewaju Freedom
Eliza Segiet
Mazher Hussain Abdul Ghani
Lily Swarn

The Poetry Posse 2018

Gail Weston Shazor * Nizar Sartawi * Hülya N. Yılmaz
Jackie Davis Allen * Caroline 'Ceri' Nazareno
Alicja Maria Kuberska * Teresa E. Gallion
Kimberly Burnham * Shareef Abdur – Rasheed
Ashok K. Bhargava * Elizabeth Castillo * Swapna Behaera
Tezmin Ition Tsai * William S. Peters, Sr.

The Year of the Poet V
October 2018

Featured Poets
Alicia Minjarez * Lonneice Weeks-Badley
Lopamudra Mishra * Abdelwahed Souayah

Bengali

The Poetry Posse 2018

Gail Weston Shazor * Nizar Sartawi * Hülya N. Yılmaz
Jackie Davis Allen * Caroline 'Ceri' Nazareno
Alicja Maria Kuberska * Teresa E. Gallion
Kimberly Burnham * Shareef Abdur – Rasheed
Ashok K. Bhargava * Elizabeth Castillo * Swapna Behaera
Tezmin Ition Tsai * William S. Peters, Sr.

Now Available

www.innerchildpress.com/the-year-of-the-poet

and there is much, much more !

visit . . .

http://www.innerchildpress.com
/anthologies-sales-special.php

Also check out our Authors and
all the wonderful Books
Available at :

http://www.innerchildpress.com
/the-book-store.php

INNER CHILD PRESS

WORLD HEALING WORLD PEACE

2018

A Poetry Anthology for Humanity

Now Available

www.worldhealingworldpeacepoetry.com

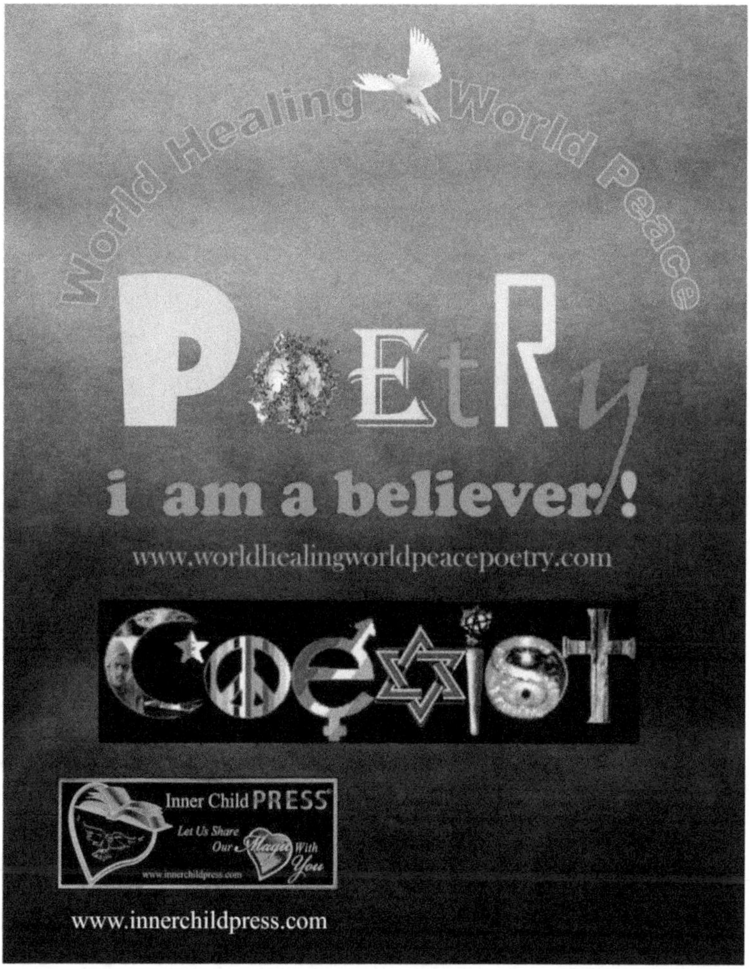

Now Available

www.worldhealingworldpeacepoetry.com

I support
World Healing
World Peace

www.worldhealingworldpeacepoetry.com

172

World Healing World Peace

i am a believer !

World Healing
World Peace
2018

Now Available

www.worldhealingworldpeacepoetry.com

Inner Child Press International

'building cultural bridges of understanding'

Meet the Board of Directors

www.innerchildpress.com

nner Child Press International

'building bridges of cultural understanding'

Meet our Cultural Ambassadors

Fahredin Shehu
Director of Cultural

Faleha Hassan
Iraq – USA

Elizabeth E. Castillo
Philippines

Antoinette Coleman
Chicago
Midwest USA

Kimberly Burnham
Pacific Northwest
USA

Alicja Kuberska
Poland
Eastern Europe

Swapna Behera
India
Southeast Asia

Kolade O. Freedom
Nigeria
West Africa

Ashok K. Bhargava
Canada

Tzemin Ition Tsai
Republic of China
Greater China

Alicia M. Ramírez
Mexico
Central America

Christena AV Williams
Jamaica
Caribbean

Aziz Mountassir
Morocco
Northern Africa

Shareef Abdur-Rasheed
Southeastern USA

Laure Charazac
France
Western Europe

Mohammad Ikbal Harb
Lebanon
Middle East

www.innerchildpress.com

This Anthological Publication
is underwritten solely by

Inner Child Press

Inner Child Press is a Publishing Company
Founded and Operated by Writers. Our personal
publishing experiences provides us an intimate
understanding of the sometimes daunting
challenges Writers, New and Seasoned may face in
the Business of Publishing and Marketing their
Creative "Written Work".

For more Information

Inner Child Press

www.innerchildpress.com

~ *fini* ~

www.ingramcontent.com/pod-product-compliance
Lightning Source LLC
LaVergne TN
LVHW051052080426
835508LV00019B/1837